PRAYERS
· FOR EVERY ·
OCCASION

Gerrit D. Schut

TYNDALE HOUSE PUBLISHERS, INC.
WHEATON, ILLINOIS

Library of Congress Cataloging-in-Publication Data

Schut, Gerrit D., date
    Prayers for every occasion / Gerrit D. Schut.
        p.   cm.
    ISBN 0-8423-4848-4
    1. Pastoral prayers.   2. Prayers.   I. Title.
BV250.S38 1992
242'.8—dc20   91-25324
                                                    CIP

99   98   97   96   95   94   93   92
10   9   8   7   6   5   4   3

CONTENTS

FOREWORD

God has given Gerrit Schut the gift of prayer words, the use of which will gladden the heart of the reader and bring glory to the Giver of the gift of the Holy Spirit and to the church of Jesus Christ.

Arranged in alphabetical order, the prayers cover every subject imaginable. They can be used from the pulpit, in Sunday school classes, during home devotional times, and for special occasions. The reader can add to what is written here other thoughts and words, but the words here will immeasurably enhance the value of the Word, promote the prayer life, and do for others what they are not able to do for themselves. Prayers for the birth of a baby, the loss of a loved one, marriage, business—you name it. They are here.

What a treasure trove it is and how useful on the nightstand before the reader sleeps and when the reader awakens at the dawning of the new day! I recommend it without reservation for the riches to be found on every page.

Dr. Harold Lindsell
Editor emeritus, *Christianity Today*

ABANDONED

Dear Father, we pray for babies and young children abandoned by irresponsible parents and for teenagers driven from abusive homes to wander hungry, cold, and penniless down dangerous streets.

We pray for families deserted by abusive fathers and for wives who are having a hard time supporting their children.

We pray for the elderly who have been deserted and forsaken, who feel the ache of isolation, and who endure the crippling confines of wheelchair and bed.

For all who *are* and all who *feel* abandoned we pray your mercy, comfort, and peace through Jesus Christ, our Savior.

Amen.

ABILITIES

Dear Father of all gifts, in comparison with others, my talents and abilities seem almost nonexistent.

Spare me from envying those whose abilities rise high against the sky of achievement while mine are stunted and nearly useless.

Teach me to do the best with what I have and to develop it to the highest degree possible for your glory.

Show me that a person will not be rewarded on the kind of talent or its great effect, but rewarded for faithfulness and commitment, no matter what the ability.

May I hear your "well done!" for what I am and have when I stand in the day of rewards.

Amen.

ABORTION

Dear Lord of all life, through the miracle of conception, you gave a life to me, and for no viable reason, I took it away!

Now, great remorse haunts me and heavy guilt plagues me. I am tormented with thoughts of what this child would be if it had had a cnance to be born, to learn, to laugh, to love, to achieve, to be married and have children, and to make me happy in my older years.

Dear God, give me peace of mind, cleanse my heart, wash my guilt away.

Perhaps, O Lord, I may meet this aborted life in the world to come, to behold, to embrace, and to love.

Amen.

ACCIDENT

Dear Lord, be with those handicapped through accidents—those disfigured, scarred, or disabled.

In their discouraging and depressing times, be their comfort and encourager.

May they see that the thorn of a handicap is often one of the greatest spurs to success.

Give them determination to develop themselves and may your strength and love inspire them to persist till they discover personal fulfillment as human beings.

Amen.

ADDICTION

Dear God, free us from the enslaving tyrannies of our addictions.

Help us who are chained by drug dependencies to see that the real cost is more than in dollars, but in poor health, shorter lives, and a heavy burden on families and society.

Forgive us for using addictions of all sorts to escape life, as substitutes for self-esteem, confidence, competence, happiness, and meaning in life.

Snap the binding chains that restrict us from being all that we can be. We are made in your image. We have a high calling. May we be worthy of it.

Help us through the power of the Holy Spirit.

Amen.

ADORATION

Dear God, if we could condense

all loveliness to one flower . . .

all music to one song . . .

all beauty to one face . . .

all poetry to one line . . .

all happiness to one moment . . .

all love to one glance . . .

it would fail to describe your greatness, holiness, love, and mercy through Jesus Christ, as a candle fails to compare with sunlight.

Amen.

AFFECTATION

Dear Lord, forgive us our affectations — for stumbling over our own bluff.

Show us that appearing to be what we are not aims a spotlight on the varnish of our hypocrisies.

May we be genuine instead of counterfeit. We may impress others by virtues we parade, but we will win them by those we possess.

Forgive us for practicing a fake personality, like veneer over our incompetence, knowing that time will expose our pretensions.

Lord, before you we are transparent as glass. May we be candid, yet tactful; honest, yet loving; open, yet with never a closed mind or heart.

Amen.

AGING

Father of eternal youth, as time's plow furrows our physical frame, may we always be young at heart.

Our hair may gray or thin, our skin may wrinkle, our bones may become fragile, our faculties may dim, but our hearts need not age unless our remorse exchanges places with our dreams.

May we never lose interest in life. May our minds ever be open to the surprises of our universe. Help our curiosities to take a daily jog through intriguing fields of knowledge.

When we reflect, may we relive the joys of the past and not be resentful over the hurts and the heartaches.

May we remember that the heart never grows old if it is touched by the Spirit of eternal youth.

Amen.

AGONY

Dear Lord, I walk alone down this twisted path of personal agony.

My heartache is too deep for expression. Often, my tears flow unbidden.

Walk with me through this darkness and be my light. Hold my hand in this echoing loneliness and be my companion. At these numbing crossroads of confused indecision, be my guide.

Create rainbows of hope in my tears with the sunlight of your presence.

Help me to hold high the lamp of faith, for someday you will help me understand the agonizing puzzles of life.

Amen.

AIRLINE PILOT

Dear Lord, as I climb high into the sky with my precious human cargo, be my pilot.

Give me alertness of mind, confidence in my training, and faith in the trustworthiness of my plane.

Protect me from dangers of the air, from mechanical malfunctions of my craft, and from the vagaries of weather.

Hold my plane in the safety of your hand as you hold soaring eagles in thermals of air.

Amen.

AMERICA

Dear Father, I thank you for this land of beauty, opportunity, and freedom.

I thank you for pilgrims sailing rough seas in small boats and setting foot on forested shores, for immigrants fleeing tyranny and poverty, and for pioneers who trekked the long trails to the West.

I thank you for flags rippling, for church and school bells calling, for bands playing on parade, and for liberty to travel.

I thank you for jobs, for opportunity to make a living, for business, for trade, and for all that makes life comfortable in our country.

I thank you for mountains shouldering the sky with muscles of rock, for redwoods towering in cool mists, for rivers twisting across the land, for flower-decked meadowlands, and for all of nature's beauty and bounty.

May we never forget the price of our freedom—of falling planes, of sinking ships, of dying men, of mass suffering.

I thank you for all that made America. I thank you for allowing me to be born in such a time as this and in such a land as ours.

Amen.

ANGER

Dear Lord of love, forgive me for losing my temper for insufficient cause and for being short-circuited without justification.

So often, what I lack in argument I make up in anger. So often, when I open my mouth in rage, my mind locks its door.

If I must express anger, may it be a humble, moral indignation against injustice and sin.

May I not hold anger long, like slow-burning coals, lest I be consumed.

At the close of each day, may I confess the wrongs of anger. Free me from the temper bursts of today. And may there be no permanent damage to those who were the unfortunate victims.

Amen.

ANXIETY

Dear Lord of peace, remind me that a small event filled with worry casts a long shadow and that most stresses lie in anticipation.

Lord, so often when I am tormented with worry I lose common sense and make impulsive decisions.

Remind me that whenever great anxieties cloud my days, you are in constant lockstep with me and that whatever I am going through you go through with me.

Help me to rise above troubling events like an eagle soaring, for an eagle never worries about crossing mountains ranges or rivers. Help me to soar in the clear air of faith.

Lord, I know that you will exchange my anxiety for your peace if I am in a bargaining position.

May I, like the birds and the flowers, live in the daily sunshine of trust in your providence.

Amen.

APPEARANCES

Lord, teach me that things as they appear to be are often deceptive.

Give me the objectivity to look deeper than what strikes the eye, for what is beautiful and true is many times hidden from view.

In the midst of fads, fashions, and the whitewash of phoniness, give me insight to weigh what has integrity and value.

Lord, you judge me by what is in my heart, for the heart is what I am.

Amen.

ARMED SERVICES

Dear Lord, the principles of freedom are obtained at great price, and our armed services are called to protect them.

In times of war, guard those who serve our country. Be next to those in submarines and ships, in planes and tanks, with those who march in infantry, and those who are in command.

When the grim news of "died in action" comes, may the survivors feel your comfort. As horrible as war is, may they have died with honor defending what is one of the most precious things on earth — the right to live in freedom.

May we realize that it is better to defend our freedom than live and die a slave under a brutal tyrant.

Amen.

THE ARTS

Dear Lord of all beauty, we thank you for the fine arts — mirrors of the mind, artistic expressions of the soul.

We thank you for stirring music, for harmonious architecture in form and function, for the chiseled exactness of sculpture, delighting the eye.

We thank you for the essence of literary inspiration embalmed in great books.

We thank you for all noble crafts that engage the mind, stir the creative imagination, inspire the heart, and please the eye.

We thank you most of all for the incomparable artistry of your love and grace expressed through Jesus Christ our Savior.

Amen.

ASTRONOMY

Dear God, we are filled with awe at the heavens.
Countless galaxies, billions of light-years away, stud the
night.

We thank you for astronomers who sit in silent
observatories studying the distant stars and planets and
communicate their knowledge to us.

Your Word says that the heavens declare your glory
and handiwork.

Our earth is but a planetary speck lost amid the
bewildering maze of suns, stars, and planets. Yet you
loved our world of spiritual need, and you touched our
world through Jesus Christ, our Savior.

Amen.

ATHLETE

Lord, help me, as an athlete, to perform my best whether I win or lose.

Teach me that heroes are sometimes born in the hour of defeat and that I am never so close to winning as when defeated in a righteous cause.

May I learn that the real goal is not reached when it is posted on a scoreboard, but when my heart has reached its goal line.

Help me to be faithful in the race of the Christian life and to finish my course with joy, for it is not the roar of the crowds that will give me honor, but the lasting trophy of your "well done!"

Amen.

ATONEMENT

Dear Redeemer, my heart bows in reverence for your redeeming grace through the atonement of the cross.

Lord, your grace saved me. There was nothing I could do to merit your salvation.

I thank you for the gift of life through Jesus Christ. *Amen.*

AWE

Dear Lord, buried deep within our hearts there exists the capacity for awe — whether a stone or a star, an insect or an elephant, a rhododendron or a redwood — each created thing has its aura of awe.

We stand in awe of a flaming sun, an atom, the anatomy of a human being, the mind, and all that is noble within the heart.

Our hearts are filled with wonder that you have reached down through space to plant a cross to save us from our sins and to bring us to heaven at last.

Amen.

BALANCE

Dear Father, each day a multitude of voices are begging us to buy, to experience, to believe, and to side with radical views and beliefs.

May we strive for balance in our lives, for most things have two extremes, and often truth lies somewhere in the middle.

Father, your universe is held together in delicate and precise balance.

Your Word instructs us how to live balanced Christian lives through the power of the Holy Spirit.

Grant us the wisdom to be balanced in most things lest we swing to extremes, appear ridiculous, and lose our effectiveness with others.

Keep us from being willfully ignorant and prejudiced concerning the other person's views, for we may miss the truth.

Amen.

BANQUET

Heavenly Father, you have blessed the soil with abundance, these tables with delicacies, and our bodies with the need for food.

If there is gaiety tonight, may it have its root in inner Christian joys.

If there is animated conversation, may it spring from fountains of caring that seek the happiness and welfare of those sitting next to us.

Guide the person speaking to us. May the words nourish our minds and stimulate our hearts as food does our bodies.

Remind us as we eat that in many places in our world hunger stalks and leaves misery and death in its wake.

We pray that as we leave we may have grown closer to one another because we have grown closer to you.

Accept our humble thanksgiving for this food. We ask that you be our honored Guest.

Amen.

BEANUTY

Father in heaven, we thank you for a secret nerve within us that vibrates to beauty.

We thank you for strands of beauty woven throughout your universe;

for fire in a sunset and twinkle in a star;

for color in a rainbow and silver in a waterfall;

for bloom in a flower and the song of the wind.

Show us that true beauty is more than the allure of bone structure, but is something deep within the heart.

Lord, we know that beauty may be an accident at nineteen, but can be the result of a beautiful life at ninety.

May we express the beauty of love, faith, truth, virtue, honesty, and sacrifice, for this is the beauty of Christ.

Amen.

BELONGING

Lord, you created us to belong. None is an island in the vast sea of humanity. As social beings, we need the company of others to make our lives fulfilled.

Be with those who are lonely for companionship within the narrow walls of their personal worlds. May they sense your presence.

Teach us to give love and friendship lavishly, for the returns will be many. Teach us the power of a smile, a kind word, a handshake, a phone call, a letter.

We thank you for spiritual bonds that bind us forever to you, our Savior and Lord.

Amen.

BIBLE

Holy Spirit, Author of the Sacred Scriptures, we thank you for the Bible,

    for its unfolding revelation of Jesus, the Son of God;

    for the diversity of its authorship;

    for the divine inspiration of its text;

    for the historical accuracy of its contents;

    for the meticulous transcription of its ancient manuscripts;

    for its message of sin's deliverance through the cross of Jesus;

    for its gateway of faith into the spiritual kingdom;

    for its hope for the hopeless, comfort for the comfortless, and mercy for the merciless;

    for its unique and divine claims, promises, and hopes;

    for the assurance of a life beyond this life.

Amen.

Dear Lord, into our lives you have given this new life filled with promise.

May he always feel safe and loved. Give us wisdom to guide him in things right. Give him a strong faith in himself, for he will need confidence for the road ahead.

Give him courage to stand tall, even if alone. May he not be judgmental, but filter all he hears through the sieve of truth.

Teach him that there is no shame in tears, and that it is not wrong to fail, only to be satisfied with it.

May he learn that contentment is true wealth.

May he never lose hope, because for every night there is a dawn.

Show him the wonder of books, the joy of music, and the loyal support of friends. Show him the glory of the stars, the mystery of birds on wing and bees in the sun.

When he reaches the road's end, may he look back and see that he never walked alone.

When age weakens our frames and dims our eyes, may we be proud of him, and may he remember us kindly.

Amen.

Dear Lord, into our lives you have given a new life filled with tomorrows. We have reserved a very special room of love in our hearts for her.

May she grow up to be beautiful in soul. May she have high spiritual ideals so she will have inner strength and courage to stand tall.

May she not believe all she hears; yet, may she not lose basic trust, for distrust is lonely.

Though she may fail, may she never be content with it, for failure need not be fatal.

May she discover the fairyland of books, the magic of good music, the power of love, and the trust of true friends.

Should she have children of her own, may she instill into them our virtues but not our weaknesses.

When life's night nears, and her children and grandchildren call her "blessed," may her heart beat with happiness and may her eyes gleam with stars.

Amen.

BIRTHDAY

Father of life, we celebrate another annual milestone in the life of this person. May this be a happy occasion for another year of learning, of experience, of growth.

Lord, it does not really matter how many milestones are reached; the heart remains forever young.

Lord, when all birthdays on earth end, we shall have an unending birthday where the celebration will be forever.

Amen.

BOREDOM

Father, forgive us our boredom, for it is with ourselves that we are bored.

If we have the eye to see and the desire to understand, everything around us has its intriguing story to tell.

Lord, the way of a bird in the air, a flower in the sun, a fish in the sea, a rainbow against a cloud—these and a million more speak eloquently of the wisdom and design of you, our Creator.

Make us interested in the needs of others. May we go on a safari of love and kindness, for every smile given, every need alleviated, every lonely life eased will pay rich returns to ourselves and ease the lives of those around us.

Amen.

BURDENS

Father, why are my burdens so heavy to carry? Why do they, like acids, corrode my joy? Why does each day dawn with clouds?

You promised rest for the heavy laden. You promised that you would share the load with me.

Walk down this tiresome road with me. Hold my hand so I can face another tomorrow. Help me when inner pain cripples my Christian walk and when my tears blur my vision.

Measure your steps with me and ease my burden till I am home at last.

I give my burdens to you and ask you to give me peace.

Amen.

BURNOUT

Dear God, so much of my soul and energy have been sapped by overwhelming demands and stresses that I have nothing more to give.

I feel drained, squeezed out of every ounce of energy, and I drag myself to do things that must be done.

Lord, I lose my creativeness, my interest, my effectiveness, and my spirit when I am burned out.

Give me the will power to select the highest priorities and say *no* to all the rest.

You are the restorer of my soul and body. Rest my mind from its whirling meaninglessness and my body from its sleeplessness.

May I find rest and healing in quietness and in the confidence of your strength.

Amen.

BUSINESS

In my business, Father, may I show as much concern for my customers as for myself. I know that the cash register and a contract are not as important as honest dealing and consumer satisfaction.

Make me see that loss of self-respect and honesty is far greater than loss of profit.

May I be conscious that you are the Chief Accountant, and that you will review my business transactions some day.

Lord, be my partner in business. Watch over all the transactions of my life.

Amen.

Lord, you promised that the rivers would not overflow us nor the fires consume us.

As we walk through these dark shadows of tragedy, help us to lean on your promise that you will not forsake us. Grant us courage and endurance to accept our present lot, and faith that your wisdom and love will sustain us. We believe that you will allow no more than what we are able to bear.

Help us to feel your presence and the integrity of your promises till we reach our journey's end.

Amen.

CALVARY

Dear Lord Jesus, it was my cross! Those were my thorns! Those nails were my nails, and the spear thrust my wound!

You took upon yourself my sins willingly to satisfy God's holiness, to mend the infractions of the broken law, and to cleanse me from my guilt.

I thank you for your love without comprehension, for your mercy without bounds, for your grace that cannot be put into words.

I thank you for reconciling me to God, for making me accepted in his sight.

I thank you for strength for the day, for hope for tomorrow, and for a coming home in heaven from which I shall never go astray.

Amen.

CAPTAIN OF SHIP

Dear Great Pilot, help me guide this ship through the whims of water and weather.

Hold the wheel with me through calm and storm, day and night, sun and mist, till I reach my destination.

You are the captain of my salvation. You will guide the ship of my soul through any earthly storm or darkness till I reach safe haven at last.

Amen.

CARNALITY

Father of holiness, we feel the downward drag of old habits, hurtful inclinations, and the cunning temptations of Satan.

Give us strength to resist. May we feel the upward lift of the Holy Spirit to practice those virtues that endure.

We recognize the lure of the world and the tug of all that is related to time.

Your Word says that the world and all its temporary goals will pass away, but they who perform your will shall abide forever.

In Jesus' name.

Amen.

CHANGE

Dear Lord, change seems the only permanence on earth.
   Everything on earth changes: mountains erode; rivers
      change course; sand dunes shift in the wind.
   Tides, seasons, boundaries change.
   Sunrises and sunsets, shores, days, months, years
      change.
   Fashions and fads change.
   Between birth and death, we change.
   But you are ever the same:
   Your promises know no breaking.
   Your love knows no lessening.
   Your mercy knows no diminishing.
   Your forgiveness knows no ending.
   We thank you, though change is part of the universe,
that Jesus Christ is the same, yesterday, today, and
forever.
   Amen.

CHARACTER

Father, your Word says that as a person thinks in the heart, so is the life.

Lord, I know that I am the summary of my conversations and the accumulation of my deeds, and that I am not necessarily what I profess.

May I remember that as the tree leans, so shall it fall.

Teach us that, like a cathedral, the building of character takes a lifetime, and that, like steel, it is forged in the fires of the years.

Remind me that I portray my character most clearly in the method of portraying another's.

Help me to model the love, courage, truth, empathy, and sacrifice of the character of Jesus Christ the Lord.

Amen.

CHARITY

Dear Lord, show us that the physical expression of charity becomes only a handout if the attitude of the heart is not charitable.

Whenever we give, may it be part of ourselves, for, in a sense, there is no true gift apart from some personal sacrifice.

Like springs tumbling from distant mountain snows, may our charity flow into the lives of others and bring about the spiritual greening of fulfillment.

Though we can take nothing with us, show us that we can send the real heartbeat of true charity ahead of us.

Amen.

CHILD KIDNAPPED

Dear Lord, few horrors match the heartrending
nightmares of children kidnapped.

Many are, this moment, in the hands of evil people.
They may be hurt, abused, hidden, or even dying.

May they somehow be rescued so they can come
home.

Amen.

CHILD'S PRAYER

Dear Jesus, I thank you for my mommy and daddy.

Help me to grow up to be the kind of person they will be proud of.

May they love me even when I sometimes do things that are wrong.

Keep me from being selfish, or rude, or unkind to my friends.

When I grow older, may I always do what is right so my parents will be proud of me.

When I grow older, may I help other people who have needs, like my mommy and daddy help me.

When I go to sleep tonight, watch over me.

I pray in Jesus' name.

Amen.

CHILDREN

Dear Heavenly Father, we thank you for the gift of children:

Children with questioning eyes and innocent faces,

children with infectious laughter and a sense of adventure,

children with a need for love and security and for boundaries of behavior,

children who ask questions that are hard to answer.

May we, as parents, show kindness without favoritism and love without partiality.

Help us lead them in your paths of truth and righteousness, for life has many pitfalls.

When the years lie heavy on our shoulders, may they remember us with respect and love.

Amen.

A CHOIR MEMBER'S PRAYER

Dear Lord, when I sing, may my heart be pure as the clear ring of a sterling bell.

May your harmony within me embrace all who sing with me so there may be harmony between us.

May the songs I sing remove the discord of my everyday life so my soul will feel uplifted.

May my singing be instrumental in bringing a soul to heaven as well as heaven to a soul.

May I not be carried away with my performance and forget a listener's deep yearning for the message in the music.

Should I receive a compliment, may I be inspired without being inflated.

Help me filter flattery for the truth it may contain, for flattery is like perfume to inhale, not to swallow.

Remind me that if I am pleased at finding fault, I will be unhappy at discovering perfection.

Keep me from being envious, for it feeds on the decay of discontentment.

Always remind me that whatever timbre my voice, I am a nightingale with you if my heart is in tune.

Amen.

Dear Lord of the church, from all nationalities, races, colors, and creeds, you call out a people for personal relationship through Jesus Christ our Savior.

We know that different churches express their religious devotion in different ways. Lord, teach us that the place and ritual of worship is not as important as the state of the heart.

Lord, your church is built upon the Rock, Jesus Christ, and the gates of hell shall not prevail against it.

We thank you that we belong to the true church by faith in Christ.

Amen.

CHURCH LEADERS

Dear Lord, you are the head of the church.

You have instructed us to elect those who are spiritually and mentally qualified to lead us as your people.

Their responsibilities may be heavy; matters of business may be many; decisions may be difficult.

Personalities may conflict, egos become inflated, and opinions become narrow.

Guide our leaders that they may show impartiality without prejudice. May all discussion be tempered with wisdom, love, and fairness. May the good of the whole church always be foremost and not the whims, power plays, or the self-interest of a person or a group.

Give them wisdom and common sense, and may they seek your will in the guidance of this, your flock.

Amen.

CIVIC MEETING

Dear Father, may we be true to this civic responsibility entrusted to us.

May our abilities measure up to issues before us. Help us to be thorough in our investigations and factual in our presentations.

Give us insight without oversight, discernment without distortion, fairness without favoritism, prescience without prejudice, and a clear conscience without compromise.

May we cultivate empathy and see that small decisions may have far-reaching effects and are of great consequence to some.

Give us strength to stand tall, even if alone, for it is better to fail in something right, than win in something wrong.

Guide this meeting and remind us that all we do here will be reviewed in the council halls of the last day.

Amen.

CLEANSING

Lord, your Word says that if we confess our sins that you will forgive them and cleanse us.

From the fountain of your mercy may the flood of your forgiving grace flow over us till we are clean before you.

Amen.

CLICHES

Father, forgive us our constant use of cliches—those overused, weary words drained of color and vibrancy.

We have the greatest message in the world and a rich language to communicate it. May we not become careless in our use of the language and slip into the rut of tired expressions.

May our language be filled with meaning, zest, and interest so that our readers and listeners will be inspired.

Help us realize that a single word may lead to the light or condemn to darkness.

We thank you for Christ, the Living Word, who communicated his eternal love to us on the cross of Calvary.

Amen.

COMFORT

Dear Lord, you are with us when we sing in the sunlight of good fortune or when we grope through the fog of depression. You are with us when our tears flow and when our hearts bleed.

You are with us when we hunger for love more than for food.

You comfort us when we are broken with guilt and racked with grief.

You understand the apprehension when we face the surgeon's knife and are confined to a bed of terminal illness.

You are with us when our children leave us and when our parents pass away.

We pray that you will shore us up with the sturdy timber of your unbreakable promises so we can stand tall in the storms of life.

We thank you for your comfort expressed in your Word.

Amen.

COMMITMENT

Teach us, Lord, that commitment is a responsible word for every Christian.

No person is totally solitary; each is related to someone in some responsible way.

May our word be our bond, and our promise a reflection of our integrity as much as is humanly reasonable and possible.

Forgive us if we deceitfully promise more than we are able to perform.

We thank you for your commitment to us through the revelation of your Word.

We thank you that Jesus committed himself to us so that we might be saved from our sins.

Amen.

COMMITTEE

Dear Father, in this room are different views, different ways of expression, different emotional intensities, and different roads that lead to conclusions.

May we combine clarity of mind with kindness of heart. May we be impartial without bending to strong personalities. May we sacrifice self-interest for the good of the whole.

Guide our discussions and decisions. May we do our work with love and with clarity of vision for the benefit of those we represent.

May your name be glorified through our efforts. In Jesus' name.

Amen.

CONCEIT

Father, forgive us the sins of big-headedness.

Puncture the inflated air of self-importance by which we deceive ourselves and others.

Show us that when we practice snobbery we indirectly flatter ourselves.

Lord, everyone is superior to us in some little way. Often, when we think we are superior, our very thinking nullifies it.

Father, if we could see what a small vacancy we may leave on earth, we will think far less of the place we occupy in life.

Teach us the art of true self-awareness. Show us that our only boast is what you have done for us through Christ our Lord.

Amen.

CONFESSION

Dear Lord, forgive us for carrying garbage bags of past failures as if they were boxes of jewels. Forgive us for wearing old habits, old hurts, and old prejudices as if they were designer clothes.

Forgive us for failing to be kind when someone was bleeding with wounds of the heart.

Forgive us for not going that extra mile when someone's load pushed him to his knees.

Forgive us for sinning deliberately, knowing the consequences.

Forgive us for expecting someone to make us happy and then being critical when the fault was within ourselves.

Make us sharp to the needs of others and to the delinquency within ourselves.

Amen.

CONFIDENCE

Dear Lord, you said that in quietness and confidence our strength would lie.

Lord, we know that fear can be fatal in many ways if we lose confidence.

We ask that you be our Rock of Ages in the shifting sands of our confusion.

Be our Good Shepherd at the crossroads of our indecision.

Be our Living Bread for the hunger of our souls.

Shine as the Bright, Morning Star down the pathways of uncertain tomorrows.

Dear Lord, confidence in your Word is half of victory. And through Jesus Christ, we are assured of winning.

Amen.

CONFORMITY

Father of truth, may we not give in to those ideologies that are contrary to the clear teachings of your Word.

Watch over us lest we become robots, allured by strange fads and cults that promise everything except truth.

Your Word instructs us that we are not to be shaped and molded to worldly ideals, but that we are to be transformed by spiritual renewal.

Give us mental acuity to sift the right from the wrong and the spiritual dedication to follow through on what is right.

Amen.

CONFUSION

Dear heavenly Father, in our confused day give us a clear head and a pure heart.

Life has so many intersections with no clear directions. Give us common sense and clarity of thinking to make proper decisions.

Help us seek the principles of your Word, the guidance of counselors, the support of friends, and the power of the Holy Spirit to help us find our way.

May we trust you one day at a time, for you will support and lead us into the light that we need.

Amen.

CONGRESS

Dear God of government, we thank you for the Congress of the United States of America.

May it be farsighted and rise above self-interest and the temptation to be less than what is ideal.

May it seek the welfare of the whole country and never engage in anything that erodes our rightful freedoms under the Constitution.

Give it a sense of deep dedication and clear direction in all of its weighty responsibility.

May it seek your guidance in making momentous decisions. May it never place power and position before the needs of the country.

We ask that you will guide and direct these elected men and women. May they always depend on your power to assist them in their responsible positions.

Amen.

CONSCIENCE

Dear Lord of moral law, we know that the only true peace is that of our inner voice—our conscience.

Higher than all courts of the land is the court of conscience.

Teach us that conscience does not ask if it is safe, expedient, popular, or socially acceptable, but if it is right.

We thank you that through the atonement of Calvary our consciences can be at rest, for through the cross we can be forgiven.

We confess our wrongs this day that our consciences may be at peace, for no grass is as green as a conscience at rest.

Amen.

COUNTRYSIDE

Dear Creator, I thank you for the beauty of the countryside—for winding roads and wooded trails, for chattering brooks and sparkling lakes, for singing winds and warbling birds, for cattle on a thousand hills, and farmlands in a thousand valleys.

I thank you for weathered homesteads full of treasured memories and for old schoolhouses where the echoes of children's laughter cling to the walls.

I thank you for lush meadows adorned in festivals of dandelions and for graceful trees turning golden in autumn.

I thank you for sounds of the barnyard, for splintered rail fences, and for corn rustling and wheat waving golden in the wind.

I thank you for the solitude of the fields, for the pink of dawn and the fire of sunset.

I thank you for all the beauty of a varied countryside and all that speaks of your majesty and design.

Amen.

CRITICISM

Father, if our skins are thin, it is difficult to accept criticism. If our heads are thick, we will not learn from our critics, for they often, with good intent, reveal our weaknesses and test our principles.

Help us to understand that troubled people make trouble, and sometimes sharp tongues and dull minds go together.

Help us remember that in a critic's life there may be deep personal wounds, failures, and frustrations that affect one's view of life.

May we learn from our critics what is true with graciousness, and rise above what is insulting or false with quiet confidence,

Remind us that a monument was never erected to a critic.

May we remember that Christ himself was criticized for truth, and he had no fault.

When we are tempted to pick away at someone, help us to say words of love, kindness, and help instead.

Amen.

CROSS

Dear Lord Jesus, your cross is the continental divide of all time.

It is the beam of your mercy touching earth.

Through a crown of thorns, nails, darkness, and unspeakable suffering, it is your plan to die in our place so that we might be spared judgment for sin.

Your cross is the source of our new birth, our new name, our new family, and our new hope of eternal life.

May we ever hold high this symbol of our new life so that we may ever die to our worldly ways and live anew in the power of your Holy Spirit.

Amen.

CURIOSITY

Dear Creator, you made a world full of mystery and intrigue. Every leaf, every insect, every star, every bird, every animal—absolutely everything has its story to tell.

May we open eye and mind. Inflame us with insatiable curiosity—this first and simplest of human emotions, this thirst of the heart and mind for knowledge.

May we realize that all that is great in our world is due to initial curiosity.

Forgive us for the terrible sin of being bored with ourselves, for then we are bored with everything else.

Amen.

DANGER

Dear Lord, danger lurks in ambush—danger of illness, of loss, of slander, of murder, of abuse, of betrayal, of plague, and of war.

Your Word says that your angel of protection watches over us. As your children, we are in the palm of your hand, and you will not allow danger to threaten us apart from your presence.

In times of danger, give us stability. In times of fear, give us peace.

Lord, danger may have its better side. It often tests us, and, if we conquer it, we become stronger. It then is greater than safety, which may leave us weak and vulnerable.

At all times, we come to you and ask that you protect us from that which would make us less effective in your service.

Amen.

DEATH

Dear Lord of life, your resurrection wrenched the iron doors of death off their rusted hinges. You gave a crushing blow to its dark and terrible reign.

We thank you for your promise of our future resurrection, that we shall rise from our graves at your call to be with you forever.

Yet, we miss those we have loved and laid to rest. Absent are their voices, their smiles, their presence.

We may have to die, but death has lost its sting! On the cross and through your resurrection you conquered it forever.

We thank you for that coming day when we shall be in heaven. There pain, illness, tears, loneliness, and despair will be no more.

Eternal peace will be in the valley, and from the oceans of your love, cool winds of comfort will soothe our fevered spirits forever.

Amen.

DECEIT

Father of truth, if we practice deceit, we are entangled in a very complicated web.

Lord, it is easy to deceive ourselves and not be fully aware of it; it is easy to deceive others and not have them discover it.

May we understand that we are easily fooled by what we love.

Lord, forgive us for practicing trickery upon others, for we have caused the greatest injury upon ourselves.

Keep us safe from the tempting traps of the Great Deceiver.

Amen.

DECISIONS

Dear Lord of wisdom, some decisions are so complex that they are hard for us to understand and handle.

We need your help.

Give us discretion as we weigh heavy issues before we decide on them. May we not act impulsively and live to regret.

May we not be afraid of deciding against the pleasant if it is in the way of the important.

Help us when it is necessary to separate the wheat of what is right from the chaff of what is expedient.

Rescue us from being slaves of indecision, for then we are slaves of frustration and stress.

Give us faith to commit our decisions to you for your glory and for our good.

Amen.

DEPENDABILITY

Dear heavenly Father, teach us that few virtues are as important as dependability. We know it is an inner honesty, a reflection of what we are.

Father, back of your Word stands your integrity and dependability. They will not change though all else does. They are reflections of your character. Your Word will not pass away though heaven and earth does.

If we are fickle and, at times, undependable, forgive our weaknesses.

Help us not to promise more than we can perform, or perform less than what we promise.

Amen.

DEPRESSION

Father of joy, I don't understand all the reasons I am depressed.

I only know I feel sad and alone, and everything seems hopeless and dark.

Uphold me with your promise that you will never leave nor forsake me. Pierce this cloud of my sadness with your shining beam of hope.

May I feel a sense of your presence in my state of melancholy.

Keep my faith strong each day so that joy and optimism, like the sunrise, will burst across the long valleys of my gloom.

Amen.

DESPAIR

Lord, so often you seem so far away, and despair, like a black cloud, sweeps across the sky of my dreams. But, I know that with you . . .

I am never too lonely to be loved . . .

never too sinful to be pardoned . . .

never too shattered to be mended . . .

never too enslaved to be freed . . .

never too bereaved to be comforted . . .

never too doubting to have faith . . .

never too old to be remembered.

Lord, lead me today, from the wasteland of my emaciation into verdant valleys of fulfillment and along sunlit streams of encouragement till I am restored and my cup overflows.

Amen.

DESTINY

Dear heavenly Father, teach me that I should never make destiny a scapegoat for my sins, but that destiny is not so much chance as it is choice.

Show me that I am responsible for what I place within the frame of my destiny.

May I understand that if I deliberately do wrong I cannot call it a dragon of destiny.

Father, I know, as I view life, that what may seem accidental to me are eternal moves in your overall plan.

Help me to submit my entire life into your hands so that my destiny will be assured and glorious.

Amen.

DETOUR

Heavenly Father, so often, in my travels, in my decisions, in my aims for the future, I face detours that upset me.

You are the God of Providence. You foresee what danger lies ahead, the inaccessible passages that would hinder or even destroy me.

Lord, often pleasant surprises lie in detours: a scenic bend in the road, time to reflect on your beauty and goodness, time to refresh myself from the hurry of life, a detour to rescue me from my own radical decisions and save me from self-destruction.

Help me to view detours with anticipation for something I have not seen or known before.

Amen.

DIRECTION

Dear God, you commanded Noah to build an ark against all common sense.

You led Abraham out of Ur of the Chaldees to a land he knew little about.

You led the Israelites across the Red Sea against great odds.

Lord, this day, I need direction for my confused mind and for my aching heart.

Give me, through your guidance, a clear sense of what to do.

If necessary, lead me step by step into the promised land of spiritual victory till the high walls of opposition fall down flat and I can claim personal victory.

Amen.

DISCERNMENT

Dear Lord, so many voices call; so many paths beckon; so many decisions taunt us.

Give us sharpness of mind, purity of motive, depth of empathy, and strength of will so we may discern what is best and carry through.

Help us through intricate issues, quicksands of the unexpected, and quagmires of sticky circumstances.

Holy Spirit, guide us through the tangled maze of daily conundrums that we may feel freed and may praise you.

Amen.

DISCONTENTMENT

Dear Lord of all serenity, show us that the root of discontentment burrows deep into the soil of self-love.

And if so, no matter how high on the rung of the ladder we climb, no matter how much we accumulate, we will never be satisfied.

Teach us that if we love ourselves inordinately, we will have less love and empathy for others.

Forgive us for being picky with others because of our own emptiness.

Show us that the basis of contentment is a right relationship with you, for that enables us to have a better relationship with others.

Whether in privation or in a palace, we can be content in heart if your peace abides within.

May we discover, like Paul, that whatever state we are in, we can learn to be content.

Amen.

DISCOURAGEMENT

Dear Great Encourager, you gave Joshua courage to conquer Canaan. You gave Daniel courage in the lions' den. You gave Elijah courage against the prophets of Baal.

In the midst of great obstacles and formidable odds you can give us courage.

In the sometimes daily desperations of life, give us the hope of encouragement. Be with us in the dark nights of our fears till the dawn appears.

Be our guide in the difficult wildernesses till we reach the promised land of personal victory through Christ.

Show us that with you, there is no Red Sea that we cannot cross, no lions' den where we cannot be safe, no storm on life's ocean where we cannot be secure.

Amen.

DIVORCE

Heavenly Father, be with those who are wounded, torn, embittered, frustrated, grieving, and lonely because of divorce.

Help children of divorced parents to adjust to the loneliness of separation. May they retain the love of parents and be assured of their constant friendship.

Somehow help those who are short of money to pay necessary expenses.

May those who carry heavy loads of guilt find release and peace at the cross of Jesus Christ who alone can give inner strength to carry on.

Amen.

DOGMATISM

Father of truth, make us see that we don't have a full revelation on everything.

Make us see that Christianity may be destroyed by bigotry as well as by apathy.

May we remember that others are not necessarily ignorant because they happen to disagree.

Force us to see that we often are the most dogmatic and arrogant on views we understand the least.

May we lay aside prejudice and always be open-minded to listen, for—who knows—there may be gold in the ore of another's heart and mind.

May we discover what truth is and then stand with assurance and without the offending attitude of dogmatism.

Amen.

DOUBT

Dear Lord, a doubting Thomas lurks within each of us at times. We yearn to have our senses satisfied.

Help us to remember that doubt is often a spur to success and, in the end, often leads to certainty.

Let us not rest on our doubts, for they are quicksand, but let us be willing to investigate till we find the rock of truth.

Clear our minds from personal prejudices and fallacies. Help us to see a subject from every possible angle, for truth is not always obvious or evident.

Help us to see that it is by the great step of faith that we find assurance of our salvation and the certainty of the world to come.

Amen.

DUTY

Dear Lord, the summary of all duty is to love you above all and our neighbors as ourselves.

Teach us that duty ignored will have its day of reckoning, but when duty is formed into a habit, it will have its hour of reward.

Remind us of our duty to our families, to our country, to our work, and to you and your Word. We know that our performance will be examined in the end.

Give us a sense of high mission so that we will be eager to perform those things required of us. May we do all our duties with a light and willing heart.

Amen.

EASTER

Dear resurrected Jesus, we thank you for that morning when the rim of the rising sun slipped above the Judean hills and you arose from death.

We thank you for the electrifying announcement of the angels that the tomb was empty.

Dear Lord, we know that the entire foundation of the Christian belief system would crumble to dust if it were not for the resurrection.

Now, when the time arrives that we must lay down and die, we know that there will be a future resurrection to eternal life for us.

May this gleam of hope shine down the path of the future and give us courage to live.

Amen.

ECOLOGY

Dear Creator, the earth is yours and its fullness. You have created within it a beautiful harmony for man and beast.

You made all things in balance—stately forests, flashing lakes, restless oceans, flying birds, and roaming animals. You created air to breathe, water to drink, food to eat, fuels to burn, metals to mine.

Yet, because of uncaring greed, our earth's resources have been polluted and decimated.

For the welfare of the human species, give us prudence in the management of our resources so future generations may not be beggared.

Amen.

EDUCATION

Dear God of wisdom, we thank you for minds eager to learn and for a world full of information.

We thank you for the essence of great minds embalmed in books and for dedicated teachers to lead the way to higher knowledge.

We thank you for every plant, bird, rock, star, atom, and for the wonderful stories each has to tell.

May we never forget that great knowledge is without a heart if it is not anchored in your Word and in your person as Creator.

Teach us that the greatest information is that we are sinners and need to be redeemed through Christ, and that he is the way, truth, and life.

We thank you for your omniscience—your wisdom, so unsearchable in its depths, so unreachable in its heights, so eternal and unchangeable in its duration.

Amen.

ELECTIONS

Dear God of responsible government, may we be patriotic in heart, loyal in practice, and informed in mind when we vote for those who claim to be qualified to lead us as a people.

If we fail to do so, we may have to endure what we have neglected to do.

Amen.

EMPATHY

Dear God of love, help me to see that if I want to be understood, I must learn to understand.

May I be willing to see through another's eye, think through another's mind, and feel with another's heart.

May I tie on another's shoes, walk in another's step, and carry another's load.

May I be willing to share another's pain, feel the sting of another's tears, and endure the loneliness of another's heart, for if I understand, I can forgive and be forgiven.

Dear Lord, we all want to be understood and loved, and we know that the best way to possess these wonderful gifts is to practice them toward others.

Give us the gift of empathy, which you practiced toward us when you gave your Son to die for us.

Amen.

ENEMY

Dear Lord, sometimes an enemy seems impossible to love.

But if we understood an enemy, we would discover suffering and inner pain.

Sometimes enemies may be helpful. They often tell the truth about us when our friends would hesitate. They often are the first to discover our mistakes so we can correct them.

May we try to understand our enemies and love them because you loved us and died for us when we were alien from you.

Amen.

ENTHUSIASM

Dear God, we know that every great movement in history was the result of enthusiasm.

May we be careful not to confuse enthusiasm with mere excitement, for one is inward and controlled, while the other is outward and often hysterical, and can quickly turn into its opposite.

Lord, may our enthusiasm for the wonders of life never wane. May it never be eroded by negativity.

Lord, we have the greatest reason for being enthusiastic, for we have the greatest message ever given and all of the gifts that go with it.

Amen.

ENVY

Dear Lord of forgiving grace, forgive us, for even the best of us are capable and oftentimes guilty of envy.

Teach us that envy is a universal sin and reveals much about what we are.

Teach us that the roots of envy reach down to the poisoned waters of discontent.

Impress upon us that envy is often harder to reconcile than hate, because, to those who envy, no fault is as bad as daring to excel.

Help us to be content with our gifts and calling in life, for then envy will have no place in our hearts.

Amen.

ETERNAL LIFE

Father of eternity, you know no beginning nor ending, and within your being you encompass all time.

You exist within your serene and holy perfection without diminishment.

We thank you for Jesus who gave his life for us, for when we receive that gift by faith, we shall live forever.

Father, though decay, disease, and death may mar our time on earth, we believe that we will enter into a land of enrichment, deathlessness, joy, and meaningful activity called eternal life.

Amen.

EULOGY

Dear Lord of life, we are gathered here to pay a final tribute to the life of this person—its essence, its achievements, and also its humanness.

Lord, we know that a person's life speaks more eloquently than anything we can say. For the life of a good person is like an underground river, secretly making the land greener.

We thank you for the influence this person has had on all the lives that were touched by its kindness and love.

We leave the final eulogy to you, for you weigh righteously and give where due.

May the good of this person leave a lasting fragrance that will outlast all memories.

Amen.

EUTHANASIA—A PATIENT

Dear Lord of life, you see me upon this bed of pain in my terminal illness. I am hooked up to all these life-support systems just to keep alive. I am barely aware of those around me. I cannot communicate with them. I want to pass into your presence with dignity.

My family knows I want to go home to heaven. May they release me from the suffering bonds of earth. Take any conflicting emotions about me away from them. Give them peace in letting me go. Take their feelings of guilt away. There is no point in making them suffer emotionally and financially to prolong what is useless to both of us.

Release my suffering. Take me home.

Amen.

EUTHANASIA—THE FAMILY

Dear Lord of life, we are created in your image with dignity. You give life and you take it away. We thank you for modern medical technology that has prolonged useful life for many years.

Lord, we wonder now about prolonging life when our loved ones are in a coma, or when they are beyond hope of recovery, and ask to die in dignity. We wonder if it is right to prolong such a life unnecessarily through life-support systems, and if our giving them release is violating the sacredness of life.

We feel the tug-of-war of indecision and its accompanying guilt, and we have a struggle with our emotions.

Lord, we are aware of the great financial and emotional burden prolonging life beyond reason puts upon those who are responsible.

Grant us the wisdom, give us the peace, the freedom from guilt and regret when we decide to release this person from suffering, or lingering beyond what is normal, to pass with dignity into your hands.

Amen.

EVENING PRAYER

Father, this day is over, the fever of life is cooled, our day's work is finished, and evening gilds the hilltops and drapes the valleys with shadows.

Everything is at rest. Earth is quiet. Moon and stars keep watch overhead.

We give this day with its golden moments and shattered dreams to you to record in the eternal record.

Tonight, give us rest of body, relaxation of mind, and peace of heart.

Now, while the black night holds sway, may we find the dawn rosy with promise, and may we be filled with praise.

Amen.

EXAGGERATION

Dear God of truth, forgive us for stretching the truth beyond its natural limitations, because we weaken whatever we exaggerate.

Help us realize that exaggeration causes others to discount the reliability of what we say.

Forgive us for bleeding words of their proper meanings and thus making them anemic.

Make us see that it is better to use understatement in some things than the opposite, for then we will be more believable.

Give us mental clarity to state things as they are and not necessarily as we may perceive them, for our own perceptions may be faulty.

Lord, may we weigh our thoughts, our feelings, and our words before we speak.

Amen.

EXAMPLE

Dear Lord, make me an example of the Christ life, so
that I may teach more by what I am than by what I say.
Amen.

FAILING POWERS

Dear Lord, I guess I'm not the person I used to be.

The miles seem longer, the hills higher, the boxes heavier, and I tire more easily.

At times I seem to wander in a fog and forget things.

When I drive, I sometimes panic and wonder why other drivers are so careless.

Since I am more confined now and my senses not nearly as sharp as in the buoyancy of youth, may I focus more on the garnered fruits of my inner life. Help me to tap the reservoir of memories to irrigate the seeds of mind and heart I have gathered through the years.

Make my heart sing during dark times, in times of illness, pain, and loneliness. May my courage be strengthened by your promises, and may my heart luxuriate in your peace.

Teach me to live one hour at a time.

May I turn the eye of faith upward and look for that day when all my failing powers will disappear in the buoyant youth of life everlasting.

Amen.

FAILURE

Lord, teach me that failure need not be final, but that it is wrong to be content with it.

Show me that it is better to fail with honor than win with cheating; that it is better to win in something small, though important, than fail in something great, but insignificant.

May I not set unreasonable goals I cannot reach nor plague myself with the parasite of perfectionism and its unnecessary stress.

Teach me also that no matter how many times I fail, to keep on trying is the secret to winning.

May I never give up on myself or on life, for I am your child and life is my opportunity.

Amen.

FAITH

Dear Lord, show us that faith is creative courage and the antidote for fear.

Faith without works is like a bird without wings.

Faith is a palm sending its taproot down to the life-sustaining water below.

Faith is a fountain, and the stream that flows from it is its life expression.

Lord, give us childlike, unwavering faith in our day of world troubles, confusion, antibiblical ideologies, and personal problems.

Give us faith that believes against all odds that your Word is true and that Christ is our Savior from sin.

May this faith bring joy and assurance to our souls as well as bringing our souls to final joy.

Amen.

FAME

Dear Lord, some of us are attracted to fame as a fly to honey.

Impress on us that fame is often as fickle as Jell-O on a moving plate, or like a weather vane turning with the whims of popular winds.

Show us that many of the famous are not really happy, and that in the end, they may be ignored and forgotten. Lord, it is lonely and difficult to step out of the spotlight into the wings for the last time.

Teach us that underneath much of the show, human needs are the same and that all feet are made of the same common clay.

May we understand that true fame is not through the news media but is a relationship with you.

Lord, any true believer is famous, in the highest sense, for he belongs to royalty, to the family of Jesus Christ. We pray in his name.

Amen.

FAMILY

Dear Father, we pray for the family—the most important unit in life.

It is a unit of close bonding, of love and security, of forming and shaping, of building fences, and seeing horizons.

We pray for dysfunctional families where abuse, hate, and tragedy stalk through the rooms, and where security, peace, and love fly out the windows.

Teach us that as the family goes, so goes our society and our nation.

Give parents wisdom, patience, and Christian ideals to care for and guide their children in ways that are right.

Guide the family through the tangled brush of secularism to walk the straight path of righteousness and truth that leads to fulfillment on earth and joy in heaven.

Amen.

FANATICISM

Dear Lord, give us discernment between blind
fanaticism and wholehearted devotion to a cause.

Forgive us if we are stubborn beyond reason and
become overheated over a small segment of truth.

Help us to be bold without being brazen, enthusiastic
without being erratic, temperate without being
thoughtless, and right without being rabid.

O, Holy Spirit, may we yield to your guidance. Help
us see every facet of a question and, whenever possible,
take a stand for or against ideologies instead of people.

Amen.

FARMER

Dear Father, bless him who turns the moist, brown furrows, who sows the miracle of seed, who waits on the whims of sun and rain, and who fills storehouses with food for the world.

As he cares for his animals, harvests his crops, and provides for his own, often through long days with tired muscles, keep him safe from accident.

May his love for the soil, seed, and seasons give him a deep inner satisfaction.

May he sense your presence in the undisturbed serenity of his fields as he ponders your creation and the deep secrets and mysteries of all growing things.

Amen.

FASHION

Dear Lord, it is so easy to be caught up with changing fashions to the exclusion of better things.

We all want to look right, feel right, conform, and be accepted.

Our feelings and views change with altering styles. What was lovely yesterday is ugly today; what was ugly yesterday is lovely today. Yet, we can be too early in fashion or too long out of it, or in the extremes of it.

Lord, we know that fashions, of whatever nature, are but of the moment, but modesty is always in style.

Help us see that we may capture someone's attention by how we look to the eye, but we maintain it by what we are in the heart.

Help us to wear those virtues that never go out of style—virtues of love, joy, peace, faith, humility, a warming smile, and a helping hand.

Amen.

FEAR

Dear Father of faith, sometimes the tyrant of fear abuses us so that we limp like cripples through our days.

Sometimes, our minds lose their reasoning powers when we fear.

Sometimes, fear leaves us exhausted with its constant stress.

Your Word says that perfect love casts out fear.

Lord, you hold the world in your hands. Help us to focus all our love upon you so that fear will no longer tyrannize us.

Teach us to trust. Then we will never be afraid.

Amen.

FEELINGS

Dear Lord, I thank you for feelings—the emotional side of life.

I thank you for emotions that express themselves in laughter, tears, enthusiasm, and awe.

Lord, show me that sensitive feelings that are thrilled by the beauty of a rose are the first to be wounded by the prick of its thorns.

Remind me that nothing is small to a person with deep feelings, and that feelings that vibrate to great pleasures also vibrate to deep sorrows.

I thank you for beauty expressed in so many different ways—a sunset flaming, music soaring, love lavishing, friendships enduring, and flowers blooming.

Dear Lord, forgive us if we have misunderstood and ignored those who have deep feelings about things.

Forgive us if we have been icily indifferent to another's pain.

Amen.

FELLOWSHIP

Dear Lord, the sweet communion of kindred spirits has no equal.

Whether in joy or sorrow, fortune or misfortune, friendly and loving relationships are sent from you.

Be with those who are lonely and friendless, who long for friendship and acceptance.

We thank you for the spiritual bond in Christ, that wonderful fellowship of the saints in the family of God.

Amen.

FIDELITY

Dear Lord, remind us that we cannot measure fidelity by its ardor, but by its constancy.

May we remember that fickleness belongs to weather and should have no place in our character.

Forgive us if we habitually promise beyond our performance.

May our words and actions reflect our Christian commitment, and may we ever be true to our trust.

Amen.

FLAG

Dear God of freedom, I thank you for our flag rippling in free winds, spangled with stars, and stained with sacrifice.

I thank you that this symbol in red, white, and blue represents millions of immigrants escaping tyranny and poverty; the bravery of pioneers rolling in wagons toward the West; farmers tilling countless acres; carpenters building sprawling cities.

Lord, this flag is a dream in color and fabric waving from a million poles to remind us that every red thread is stained with some sacrifice to make this land what it is.

Bless our land, and make it a great, shining light of peace, safety, freedom, and opportunity—a heritage for all the world to see.

Amen.

FLATTERY

Dear Lord, may we distinguish between flattery and appreciation—one is from the lips, the other from the heart.

Show us that our need for affirmation or our indulgence in self-love determines our susceptibility to flattery.

Make us see that few can live up to the glowing tributes of flattery, but that all of us have feet of clay, no matter what kind of shoes we wear.

May we weigh what we hear on the scales of experience and not let it all go to our heads.

Give us true self-worth through a relationship with you so we will be immune to flattery.

Help us to see that flattery is like perfume—to smell, but not to swallow.

Amen.

FORGIVENESS

Dear Father, we ask forgiveness for being unwilling to forgive others when asking for it ourselves.

Forgive us for trying to rationalize wrong into right by twisting our consciences.

Forgive us for disagreeing in a disagreeable way.

Forgive us for seeking the spotlight of self-adulation when we are too flawed to be revealed.

Forgive us when opportunities to be kind knocked at our doors and went weeping away.

Forgive us for not living up to our capacity as your children.

Your Word says that if we confess our sins you will cleanse us from all unrighteousness.

Amen.

FOURTH OF JULY

Dear Father, we thank you for Independence Day and for all that it means.

For Pilgrims tossing in small ships on a vast sea to unknown shores.

For millions of immigrants filled with dreams and daring, with stars in their eyes and hope in their hearts.

For the freedom to speak, write, worship, travel, and for opportunity and equality.

For the beauty of our country—for rushing streams and quiet lakes; for a desert's empty stretches and a mountain's tumbled terrain; for cities sprawling across the flatlands and for hamlets nestling among the hills; for Yosemite, the Smokies, great fir forests, and tall redwoods.

May we never forget the blood of our soldiers mingling in furrows of old fields, of planes falling from the sky, of ships sinking in distant seas, of all our honored dead whose names are inscribed on stone and in memory.

Amen.

FREEDOM

Dear Author of freedom, free us from the penitentiary of our sins, from the handcuffs of guilt, from the prison of hopelessness, and from the high walls of our fears.

Unlock the doors of our selfish cells and free us into the open and flowered fields of spiritual deliverance.

Deliver us from our heart's rebellions so we can bow at your feet.

Unlock us from the narrow rooms of our limited visions, and let us roam under the open sky of spiritual horizons.

Lord, your Word says that your truth can make us free. And if so, we shall be free indeed.

Amen.

FRIENDSHIP

Dear Father, I thank you for the priceless gold of a fine friendship.

I thank you . . .

that time and distance do not change true friendships,

that most friendships are based on terms of equality,

that a trusted friend is like a flawless diamond.

I thank you . . .

for true friends who know all about us and love us anyway,

for true friendships that are, in a sense, two souls in one body,

for fine friendships that are love without wings.

We remember that Jesus said that we are his friends if we do whatever he commands us. May we be his true friend, so that it will be easier to be friends with others.

Amen.

FULFILLMENT

Dear God, you have given each of us a desire and capacity for fulfillment. Each is searching for it in different ways.

Show us that true fulfillment of spirit and soul is through Jesus Christ from whom all streams of completeness flow.

Forgive us for being sidetracked by things of little consequence lest we miss the great pulsations of our purpose and destiny.

May we not be so enslaved in a monotonous rut of self-enslavement so we miss the spell of a sunset, a strain of lovely music, the song of a bird, the sweetness of love.

Help us weigh what is important, for our worth is measured by those things about which we busy ourselves.

Lord, we are aware that we are most attracted to those things most like ourselves. Help us turn to those high values that outlast time and whose benefits lift others on the potholed road of life.

Amen.

FUNERAL

Dear Lord of life, we are assembled to lay this loved one away in a final resting place.

You gave life, you sustained it, and now you have taken it away.

As a seed is planted in the soil to die, to awake with the kiss of the sun and the softening of the rain into a lovely flower, so, like a seed, we give this body back to the ground to await the glory of resurrection.

May your presence comfort those who mourn and those whose minds are filled with memories of past years.

May they find peace in your all-wise providence.

Perhaps soon we will hear the trumpet sound, and the dawn of eternal life will slip over the hills of time, and we shall be together at last. In Jesus' name.

Amen.

FUTURE

Father of unknown tomorrows, the next bend in the road, the next letter, the next phone call may make us happy or make us sad.

Tomorrow's apprehensions often steal today's serenity and joy.

You give us just a day at a time with its responsibilities. But along with it, you give a promise of your love and care.

You watch over the hopping sparrow. You array the fashion of flowers. You give to everything that lives its daily bread.

Give us this day an innocent, childlike trust in you, for therein only lies peace.

You have provided for our yesterdays; you are with us today; you will watch over us for all the tomorrows.

Lord, help us to place all the perils of the future into your hands. And place your special blessings of this day into ours.

Amen.

GIVING

Dear Giver of every perfect gift, you gave to the void a universe; to earth all life; to mankind your image.

You gave Jesus Christ to save us, the Holy Spirit to guide us, and your Word to instruct us.

Teach us that when we give, we receive, and that which we keep, we lose.

Show us also that what we get out of life is usually in direct proportion to what we put into it.

Give us the grace to give love to our enemies, tolerance to our opponents, forgiveness to those who wrong us, friendship to the lonely, good examples to our children, and love to you.

Dear Lord, show us that when we give out of our abundance it is not as much as if we give out of personal sacrifice.

Accept the gifts of our love.

Amen.

GLORY

Dear Lord of all glory, heaven is full of your glory—of the splendor of your being, of angel song, and celestial harps.

The universe proclaims your glory—the winds sing their songs through the leaves; tumbling streams chatter your praise; blooming flowers display your beauty; birds warble your bounty.

Your glory is revealed in the person of Jesus Christ—in his love and compassion, in his miracles, in his sacrifice, in his living in our hearts.

I pray that you will rescue us from the mundane and the dreary plod of life and fill our lives with the glory of your grace.

Amen.

GOALS

Dear Lord, may we not aim too low lest we fail to measure up to our capacity. May we not aim too high lest we flounder in incompetence.

Make our personal goals the highest development of our gifts. Help us to design them so others in need will benefit.

Help us, like Paul, to press toward the goal of our high calling in Christ.

At the end of life, may we not feel remorse for not reaching those goals required of us.

Amen.

GOD

Dear God, your greatness is everywhere in your creation.

Your voice is in the roar of the surf and in the shock of the thunderclap. The drifting clouds are the dust of your feet. The galaxies are but shifting sands on the shores of your boundlessness.

Your beauty flames in the tail of the comet and twinkles in distant stars.

Your glory is revealed in a rose flaring, a sunset flaming, a waterfall glistening, and a diamond gleaming.

Yet, you number the hairs of our head and count the tears on our cheeks.

Lord, we thank you most of all for the beauty and glory of our salvation, for the golden sunrise of hope, and for the rock-ribbed promises of your Word.

Amen.

GOOD-BYES

Dear Lord, sometimes good-byes are easy to say. Sometimes they are hard. Emotional partings seem a foretaste of death, and coming together a resurrection.

It hurts to say good-bye to those we love. It hurts, we die a little, and leave behind a bit of ourselves. Tender good-byes often leave memories as vivid as bright light, a lump in our throats, and love that still flames away in our subconscious.

May we see that eventually we say good-bye to everything and everybody, for nothing is for sure, and nothing stays the same on earth.

Lord, when the time comes for us to say good-bye, may those whose lives we have touched be thankful that we were ever born.

Amen.

GOOD FRUIT

Dear Lord, you are the vine. We are the branches.

We are interdependent with you and need you to give us life. You need us, the branches, to express your glory in fruit.

In the deserts of our human needs, may we drink deep from the springs of your grace.

Prune away all that prevents us from producing the best fruit. Remove the scabs of self-interest, the worms of resentment, and the rot of lukewarmness. Make us usable and desirable to those around us.

On the clustered vines of life, help us bear the ripening fruit of the Spirit through the sunlight of your Word.

Amen.

GOOD WORKS

Heavenly Father, teach us that good works consist not so much in the outward things that we do as much as in the inward state that we are.

Instruct us that good works are love in action: carrying someone's burden, sharing someone's sorrow, and loving our neighbor.

Lord, the best kind of good works are the little, nameless, unremembered acts of kindness.

Show us, we pray, that good works can never merit our salvation, but that, like a fountain, they flow from the inner being of our personal regeneration.

Amen.

GOSSIP

Dear Lord of truth, forgive us our loose tongues that sometimes wag without being motivated by kind thinking.

May we always speak out of kindness and understanding, helping others instead of cutting them down.

Through the malicious tongue many have been robbed of hope, slandered, rejected, and often sent to premature graves.

Through your power help us to speak always the truth with kindness, for you will weigh all that we have said at the close of our lives.

Amen.

GRADUATION

Dear Lord, we thank you for cap and gown, for pomp and circumstance.

May those who graduate see that learning does not stop with a diploma.

May they dip deep into the reservoir of knowledge through the years to make a better world, a better country, a better home, and a better life.

Help them to realize that all true learning and knowledge is based on your Word and in a relationship with Jesus Christ.

Amen.

GRATITUDE

Dear Lord, we lift our hearts to you for all you have, in a thousand ways, done for us.

May we always be grateful instead of greedy. May it never be a veiled desire of receiving a greater benefit. May we never abuse it.

May our hearts sing unceasingly along with the Psalms in lifelong gratitude for your grace and mercy, salvation and hope.

Amen.

GREED

Dear Father of contentment, we can be content with little and discontent with much.

Should we be covetous, forgive us, for this is a corroding acid that eats the heart out of contentment.

May we beware if at the end of life our pockets are full and our souls are empty.

Forgive us also if we have just material wealth to leave to our heirs rather than a spiritual legacy.

Lord, may our latter years be rich in heavenly treasure, for avarice is a common sin of old age.

May we experience the treasures of love and compassion, which are the truth wealth of the soul.

May we never measure our worth by bankbook or clink of coin but by the never-eroding riches of grace through Christ, our Lord.

Amen.

GRIEF

Dear God of comfort, like a blow in the night, grief has fallen into my life. I know not where to turn. I feel an unspeakable loss and an empty loneliness. The voice I have loved is silent, a presence no longer with me. Now, there is only emptiness and blinding tears.

Dear Jesus, you understand my personal Gethsemane. You wept at Lazarus's tomb and over Jerusalem. You are the healer of broken hearts.

Walk with me through these days of my aloneness with the warm touch of your companionship.

In the silence of my room, may your promise of hope ring in my heart that someday we will meet again.

Amen.

GUIDANCE

Dear Good Shepherd, like a confused, lost lamb I come to you.

Guide me to green pastures that feed my soul and beside quiet waters that quench my thirst.

Guide me in righteous paths, for so often the ways I choose are self-serving and disappointing.

Restore my soul from the relentless scrabble of life, and teach me the art of simplicity and solitude.

In days that are dark, be my light. In my lonely times, be my companion. In days when I am afraid, support me with your eternal promises. In days of personal loss, comfort me. In days near life's end, be my hope and joy.

Amen.

GUILT

Dear Father of forgiveness, I believe that guilt is the most sensitive nerve of sorrow, and I wish I could turn time back and set things right.

Father, I know that I cannot sin with impunity, and that from a single wrong deed ghostly fears can torment me.

Cleanse my conscience from guilt through the sacrifice of Christ. May I experience that sweet peace of your forgiveness.

Amen.

HABITS

Dear Father, we know that forming habits is one of the deepest laws of human nature, and it is difficult in a moment to get rid of a lifetime habit.

We ask that you help us to be freed from wrong habits that began as innocent cobwebs and ended as cables.

May the power of the Holy Spirit give us strength and the will to turn bad habits into those that are good.

Amen.

HANDICAP

Dear Father, give me the willpower and the patience to accept my handicap as a spur to success in spite of my limitations.

You understand I cannot do what others do. You understand my embarrassment at times.

Help me to go on in spite of difficulties, for no handicap is as great as giving in to failure.

Amen.

HAPPINESS

Father of all joy, show me that true happiness is an attitude, a way of traveling, and not a distant destination. It is not the so-called greener grass beyond the fence; it is watering the grass on our own side.

Lord, it is possible to be happy with little if my heart is in tune with you. And I can be unhappy with much if my heart is centered on what I own.

Lord, may I experience the joy that never abates no matter what the circumstances are, because it is centered in a relationship with you.

Amen.

HARDSHIP

Dear Father of strength and hope, life itself is often long years of hardship, and it is my response to it that determines my ability to succumb to it or surmount it.

Lord, you can work through adversity to expose my hidden strengths and qualities that I did not know existed.

Show us that, although prosperity may attract friends, adversity weighs them and reveals whether or not they are true friends.

May I, like Job, become like pure gold when I have passed through the fires of hardship.

Lord, may the rigorous school of my own difficulties qualify me to be empathetic with those who are passing through difficult times.

Amen.

Dear Lord of love, forgive us for habits of hating that, like a contagion, poison our whole view of life.

Forgive us for stooping to the coward's revenge for being intimidated.

Teach us that the price of hating is loving ourselves less.

Help us to steer our lives by the stars of compassion, or we will never reach the haven of a tender heart.

May the incomparable love of Calvary, like a cleansing stream, wash across the barren flats of our negative emotions so that the flowers of love, kindness, and peace will bloom.

Amen.

HEALING

Dear Great Physician, we thank you for the gift of healing that lies within the body, for the person who has health has hope, and the one who has hope has everything.

Lord, teach us that true and total healing includes healing of the soul, of attitudes, and of relationships.

Lord, we may be whole in body but sick in soul and spirit.

Help us to ask for your touch of healing to establish a right relationship with you, for from that source other healings flow.

We ask this in your name.

Amen.

Dear Lord, deep within the human spirit there throbs a longing for a life beyond.

We long for an eternal life—a life free from all earthly limitations and entanglements, all that restricts from all that we aspire to be.

We yearn for a life, beyond this one, of incomparable deep dimension, a life rich and free, a life beyond the expression of human language.

Lord, your Word expresses such a place for all who have been redeemed.

There no night will darken the sky. No war will ravage the land. No disease will maim and destroy. No loneliness will isolate, and no love will grow cold.

With you, in heaven, no despair and desperation will invade. There, with you, fear and frustration will be alien, and grief and loss will be strangers.

Lord, beyond all the wonders of that world to come, we will see your face, and that will be heaven itself.

Amen.

HOLY SPIRIT

Father, we thank you for the Holy Spirit, our Comforter.

Your Word says that he will be ever present with us through all kinds of circumstances.

He will empower us, encourage us, pray for us before your throne, and minister your Word to us.

Your Holy Spirit will convict us of sin, give us strength in our weakness, and illumine our minds to the truth.

We pray that, from the branches of our lives, the Spirit may produce the fruit of a beautiful life in the hungry, desperate wastelands of our world.

Amen.

HOME

Dear Father, in all the world, there is no place like a home where love reigns, where peace pervades, and where happiness and laughter are the atmosphere.

Lord, we know that we may search the world over to find what is dearest to us, but we will return home to discover it at our own fireside.

Lord, be our permanent resident in the home of our hearts, our protector, our joy and our hope, till we enter at last into our home everlasting where all the fractious dissents of earth will be absent.

Amen.

HOMELESS

Dear Lord of the homeless, while we find refuge in homes of our own, may we not forget those who have none.

Many find their homes on the streets, in parks, in cheap rooms, under bridges, and on the shore.

Some are young, some are old and ill. A terrible helplessness overcomes some. Others have lost jobs and have no place to go.

Lord, somehow, may they find a safe and warm place, enough food, clothes to wear, proper education for their children, and jobs to support themselves.

May they experience your presence while they push their carts filled with a few belongings. Help them, in Jesus' name.

Amen.

HONESTY

Dear Father of truth, help us to always be true to ourselves, then we cannot be false to others.

May we always keep our promises whenever possible, and never promise more than we can keep.

Help us to be on guard, for there are legal ways to be dishonest.

May we be straightforward with tact, and honest with kindness.

May we always remember that honesty as well as dishonesty reflects our integrity and character.

May our words be seasoned with the salt of truth. *Amen.*

HOSPITALITY

Dear Father, your Word says that we should extend hospitality to strangers, for we may be entertaining angels unawares.

Show us that in the most common of ore, there is gold.

Amen.

HUMILITY

Dear Lord, teach us the fine art of true humility.

Show us that a feigned meekness can be a false front for malice and a mask for pride.

May we understand that humility is a correct estimate of ourselves as we are before God.

Forgive us if we become proud for our so-called humility, for this is self-conceit before you.

Amen.

HUMOR

Dear heavenly Father, because of an inner joy, we can delight in the lighter side of life. We know that laughter heals like a medicine.

We realize that often a true word is spoken in fun. If it is instructive to us, may we take it to heart.

May we see the humorous side of ourselves, for sometimes there is much to laugh at.

Show us that good, clean humor has its basis in contentment, and it makes the day more enjoyable.

Forgive us if we use humor to hurt others, for it reflects an uncompassionate side of ourselves.

Amen.

HUNGER

Father, you make grains grow across the fields and vegetables in gardens. You are the Creator of seasons, soils, and seeds.

Yet, much of our world goes to bed hungry at night. Millions are undernourished and ill, and this very minute many are dying from lack of food.

May we, as a great nation of productivity, not forget those who, because of famine and war, cannot provide for themselves.

Be with those who hunger in soul for the Bread of Life. Grant them the grains of contentment and the fruit of peace through Jesus Christ, our Living Bread.

Amen.

HURTS OF LIFE

Dear Father, life seems so unfair in so many ways to me. I am so sensitive and get hurt so easily, and never seem to heal, and then I am hurt again.

Help me to understand that those who hurt me may be full of hurt within and may be angry at life. Prevent me from having too thin of a skin in the thick of life.

Make me a healer for all who are hurting. Everyone carries a private agony in the heart. Help me to minister the salve of your love and caring to the wounds of others and then perhaps my own will heal.

Lord, I know you understand how I feel. Help me to be absorbed in the hurts of those around me; then perhaps my own sensitivity will be less. May I be willing to walk in another's shoes; then perhaps I will forget how my own shoes hurt.

Amen.

HYPOCRISY

Dear Lord, forgive us our hypocrisies, for they are mere prejudices wearing a halo.

Sometimes, before others we appear to be what we are not, but before you we are as transparent as glass.

Peel away our painted pieties, our masks and masquerades, our veneers and vanities. Forgive us if we hide behind the stained windows of religious pretensions.

Touch the paralysis of our spiritual lameness. Correct our shortsightedness that squints at another's defects but ignores our own. Cure the deafness that will not hear the cry of another's pain.

Help us to be genuine before you. Then we will appear the same before others.

Amen.

IDOLATRY

Father, we are of a modern technological age, yet in many ways we are like pagans of old.

We do not worship carved stone images in ancient temples, but we worship money, affluence, ownership, power, position, and, in many ways, we make science the god of our day.

Forgive us our idolatries. Lord, anything we place before you is an idol. May we worship you alone, for you are worthy.

Amen.

ILLUMINATION

Dear Father of light, for the darkness of our
understanding, give us light.

In the gloom of our depressions, give us light.

In the indecision of our choices, give us light.

For our searching for the truth, give us light.

In our groping in the darkness to find our way, give
us light.

For our last journey through the shadows, give us
light.

Through Jesus Christ, we pray.

Amen.

IMAGE OF GOD

Father, you have created us in your image; forgive us for creating you in ours.

Help us reflect your image in us, for we are shaped and molded by what we love.

If we are tempted to parade our piety, remind us that the worst fault is to be conscious of none.

If we are tempted to compromise truth, remind us that we weaken whatever we exaggerate and nullify whatever we distort.

May we ever follow the principles of your image as exemplified in Jesus Christ.

Amen.

IMMORTALITY

Lord of life eternal, our very being vibrates with the music of immortality— the deathless life to come. In our deep yearnings and fondest dreams we want to live forever.

Lord, in an unknown dimension of expression, in an atmosphere of buoyant health where sin and death are absent, we shall discover ultimate fullness of being.

We thank you for the words of Jesus who promised eternal life by faith in him.

May this shining hope buoy us on the troubled seas of life till we land safe in the harbor of heaven.

Amen.

INCARNATION

Dear Father of our Lord Jesus Christ, on a star-studded night long ago you commissioned your son Jesus to enter the human race, to become one of us, yet sinless.

On an earthquake-wrenched night that Son was crowned with twigs of thorns, nailed to a stake of wood to suffer for our sins.

We will ever be grateful that the Word became incarnate that we might be received into the spiritual fellowship of the family of God.

Amen.

INGRATITUDE

Dear Lord, you have showered us with homes, families, friends, food, places to worship, education, and all that we need to live a happy and secure life.

But, forgive us the sin of ingratitude, of forgetting to be thankful, of taking everything for granted.

May we never forget that all that we enjoy was purchased at the price of many lives lost.

Remind us that all that we enjoy in the spiritual sense was purchased at the price of Calvary.

Amen.

INSULT

Lord, few things are more difficult to forgive and forget than insults.

Give us wisdom and tact to handle them. May we have enough self-confidence to ignore them and enough self-worth to not let them ruin us.

Let us, when necessary, detect a bit of truth hidden in an insult so we may better ourselves.

Help us not to respond in kind, for that is not the spirit of Christ.

Amen.

INTEGRITY

Father of integrity, help us to be true to you, for then we can be true to ourselves, and true to others.

Your Word says that if we are faithful in small things we will be in great things, and if we are unjust in little we will also be in much.

Show us that integrity without knowledge is weak, and knowledge without integrity is dangerous.

We thank you for the wonderful assurance that back of your promises lies your faultless integrity.

Amen.

JOY

May we, O God, experience that deep, unperturbable joy that flows underneath like an underground stream from a distant mountain.

Spare us the temporary lows and highs of mere excitement that flare one hour and subside the next.

Lord, we believe that the most profound joy is tranquil and is apt to be silent.

Show us that joy and peace are twins, and one cannot exist without the other.

In all circumstances of life, may this joy burn with a steady glow, for you are the eternal source through Jesus Christ.

Amen.

JUDGING

Dear Lord of fairness, help us to have as sharp an eye for our own flaws as for those we judge.

Forgive us, for many times, there is a false pride in unfairly judging others.

May we never judge another unless we have walked in that person's shoes and worn that person's coat.

If judgment is necessary, may it be with kindness, tact, and truth for the betterment of the people judged.

Amen.

LANGUAGE

Dear Lord, we thank you for the gift of language and its expression in communication.

Help us to be careful how we dress our thoughts. May we do it in clear and precise style.

Preserve us from trite expressions, filler words, and sounds that have no meaning, but are habits and pauses for deficient thinking.

Help us to use the best of language in the expression of the greatest message of all — that of the eternal Word becoming part of mankind that he might take away our sins.

Father, often our emotions run deep and there seems no language for it. But you understand what we feel, and you will answer.

Lord, no language on earth is adequate to express your greatness, holiness, and love.

Amen.

LAW

Dear Lord of all law, your universe is held together by law. Nature obeys its commands. Our bodies would not exist without law.

Within the conscience, you have implanted a moral law.

Yet, you have given us a will to choose. To choose the true and the right. To choose good or evil.

Father, we know that law reveals sin and unworthiness, but it cannot correct it.

We thank you for your grace and mercy revealed in Christ, which saves us by faith apart from any merits of the law.

Amen.

LIFE

Dear Lord, I thank you for the great complex mystery of all life.

Show us that life is the most precious commodity we have. It is too wonderful to waste. We cannot save or hoard it; we must use it and never abuse it. We don't kill time; it kills us in the end.

Lord, life is not necessarily over when we die, but it is what dies within us while we live.

Help us to invest in those things that outlast life, in those things that never become obsolete.

We thank you for the quality of eternal life through Jesus Christ, our Savior. We thank you that this life is rich and deep and eternal, and that it will never go out of style.

Amen.

LISTENING

Dear Lord, in the often overriding desire to tell our own stories, teach me the fine art of listening.

Lord, we learn to understand others better when we listen.

May we listen with our eyes as well as with our ears—for facial expressions, body language, muscle and eye movements—so we may better know one another, for this is the way of loving and learning.

Give us all the patience to listen as if the words will be the last uttered, for we are traveling together on planet earth, and we only have a moment with our companions.

Dear Lord, we know that whenever we call upon you, you are always listening to the cry of the heart.

Amen.

LIVE ALONE

Dear Lord, I live alone. As time goes on, my world gets smaller. Sometimes loneliness creeps in, and I am discouraged.

Teach me that one day at a time is the best way to live, and that is how you take care of your world.

Keep me from harboring resentments or envy against those more fortunate. Keep my mind pure, my heart kind, and my actions unselfish.

Spare me from fire, thieves, from fear and the evil tongue.

When sickness comes, may I not give up hope. When I am feeling low, lift my heart with an old song.

Show me that, even though age may weigh heavily on my body, my heart never grows old.

Show me that there can be beauty in solitude and that I can be happy with simple things.

Most of all, dear Lord, surround me with your presence so that I will feel loved and secure.

Amen.

LONELINESS

Dear Lord of comfort, no person is an island surrounded by open sea, but each is a social creature and needs someone.

Be with those who are lonely, with those who live alone, whose boundaries are four walls of a room and a few treasured trinkets.

Father, we realize that deep loneliness is a naked terror, and that we sit at the windows of our own prison and cry for someone to love us.

Help us to try to build bridges into other lives instead of walling them out. Help us to reach into another's lonely life so that our own loneliness may disappear.

Yet, Lord, loneliness has produced some of the greatest music, the finest art, the best literature and poetry.

Place your loving arms around all those who are lonely and comfort them with your comforting presence.

Amen.

LOSS

Dear Father, give us the insight to see that no loss is so great but that there can be some gain.

Make us aware that it is not necessarily how much we lose, but how much we have left that is important.

Show us that all life is change, and that loss is change.

Show us from your Word that the greatest of all losses is if we should gain the whole world and lose our own soul.

May we, like Paul the apostle, count all things but loss that we may win Christ.

Amen.

LOVE

Dear Lord of love, love is the eternal essence of your being and is the deepest and most wonderful of emotions of the human heart.

Teach us that we are shaped and formed by what we love. May we learn that love based on beauty dies when beauty fades.

Dear Lord, true love is always considerate. It never keeps records of wrongs. Make us see that love is a complex maintenance of integrity in relationships and places its own happiness in the happiness of another.

We thank you for the beauty of your love. It has no bounds, it is as mysterious as eternity, as high as heaven, and reaches its warm arms to every human being.

Amen.

LYING

Dear Lord of truth, give us discernment to distinguish between lying and inaccuracy.

May we realize that our greatest punishment when we lie is not that we are not believed, but that we cannot believe anyone also.

Help us to see that a single lie can destroy our reputation for integrity.

Make us see that half-truths are also lies. Forgive us for keeping silent when we should speak, for often the cruelest lies are told at such times.

Lord, your Word says that we are to speak the truth in love. May we remember that our words reflect what we are.

Amen.

Father in heaven, help me, as a manager to expect of myself the same high standards I expect of those under me.

May I always be reasonable, impartial, and fair. May I never favor one or abuse another unfairly, for we are all equal in your sight.

Remind me that each employee needs praise, affirmation, self-respect, and love as I do.

Help us, as a group, to have a lighthearted team spirit as we work together. Give us a sense of purpose and fulfillment, and may we always be sensitive to the needs of each other.

Lord, we all have value in your sight measured by the Cross, and we are coworkers in your kingdom.

Amen.

MANNERS

Dear Lord, teach us that good manners are reflections of good breeding.

Make us see that good manners are simply making others feel comfortable.

Today, instruct us that our treatment of others reflects our relationship to you.

Remind us that courteousness is based on love of others.

May our good manners always be sincere because our hearts are caring.

Amen.

MARRIAGE

Father in heaven, we know that within the small circle of a wedding band treasures or torments can lie.

Lord, a marriage can be a harbor in a storm or a storm in a harbor. It can be a wonderful, charming relationship, or else wedlock can be a padlock.

Show us that a good marriage is making small sacrifices with love and cheerfulness.

Deliver us from ever looking for perfection, for no one can ever be perfect, least of all, we.

Lord, remind us that love endures when it falls in love with the loveliness of the soul rather than with face or body.

Show us that the ideal marriage is a marriage between an ideal husband and wife.

Teach us that when two people make Christ the center of their marriage, it is built on a spiritual foundation that will last the years.

Amen.

MATERIALISM

Dear Lord, spare us from the baited trap of materialism — this shortsighted scrabble that blocks out the sunlight of our souls.

All material things change and pass away, and the aspirations of our souls are never satisfied with the mundane.

Though we need and appreciate those things in life that provide for us, sustain us, and make us comfortable, may they never be the center of our heart's desire.

Your Word says that the world is passing away with all its inordinate desires, but they who do your will abide forever.

May we worship you instead of bowing down to gods that will forsake us when we are sick and dying.

Amen.

MEDIOCRITY

Dear Lord, deliver us from the menace of mediocrity. There are high mountains to climb, high peaks to scale. Give us the zest to reach the highest levels of our capacities.

You have given each of us the ability to excel. Help us to develop it to its maximum.

May we never be satisfied with the ordinary, for these regrets will follow us to our graves.

O, Holy Spirit, give us the will, the ability, the eagerness to do our best, for some day before you we will have to give account.

Amen.

MEMORIES

Father, I thank you for memories—those safaris into yesteryear.

Some memories are rainbowed with happiness; others tinged with sadness.

Some warm our hearts still with childhood adventures. Some are filled with awe with the wonders of the natural world.

Dear Lord, cleanse our heart of memories that are unpleasant that we may not be held back by remorse and guilt.

Fill our heart with high thoughts each day so that in old age we may have a beautiful garden of flowered memories to wander in.

Amen.

Dear God of mercy, your mercy is unchangeable and everlasting. It reaches down to our deepest needs—our sins, our fears, our lonelinesses. It flows, a sparkling stream, across the deserts of our wasted years.

Lord, though all things change, your mercy remains the same toward us.

Give us the courage and the compassion to minister mercy even to those who are merciless.

Amen.

MINISTER

Dear Father of ministry, I have one of the toughest jobs in the world. The lost, the lonely, the angry, the dispirited, the desperate, the critical sit in my pews.

Give me concrete convictions not subject to compromise on things that really matter, but make my opinions flexible.

Lord, I know I have feet of clay and am subject to fatigue, burnout, failure, and discouragement. I fight doubt, depression, loneliness, and temptation. Sometimes I must handle dull minds and sharp tongues.

Give me good self-esteem in this house of glass in which I live.

May Christ ever be my model; the Bible, my blueprint; good books, my teachers; my sermons, sharpened tools in the hands of the Spirit.

Help my ministry to cushion sorrow, dispense encouragement, build faith, repair hope, and restore love.

Help me to believe in beauty, serenity, humility, tolerance, forgiveness, and all the gifts of grace.

When I preach, may I see eyes shining with hope, hearts ringing with peace, and lives harnessed with purpose.

Amen.

MISSIONARY

Dear Lord of love, you have called me on a great mission—that of spreading your gospel in this needy place.

Grant me good health and protect me and my family from serious diseases.

May my family never suffer privation because of lack of financial support.

Lord, the work often seems fruitless and the hours are long, and often loneliness for familiar faces at home haunts me. I ask that you be my support with your abiding presence.

Help me not to give up when there is no immediate harvest, for seeds of truth need time to germinate and grow.

When the Great Reaper calls and my work is finished, may I have been faithful in my work and have done my best. If it please you, may many souls have been garnered into your kingdom.

Amen.

MISSIONS

Dear Lord of missions, missions are everywhere—on foreign fields and at home, across our own streets, down the next alley, up the boulevards, down on the farms, in towering skyscrapers and in lowly back ways of our world.

Show us that our mission field is anyone in need, anyone who is without Christ.

Empower those who are true witnesses of the truth wherever they may be found.

Amen.

MONEY

Dear Father, teach us that money is a good servant but a severe master, and that the inordinate love of it is evil. It then becomes a good and a supposed answer to fulfillment and happiness on earth.

Lord, I know that money itself does not corrupt anyone any more than good food does; it only reveals the potential corruption that was always there.

Forgive me if I have spent too much time and energy in the acquisition of things and reaped the hollow reward of emptiness in the end. You said in your Word that it will profit little if I gain the whole world and, in the end, lose a soul.

Show me that money can buy a house but not a home, medicine but not health, companionship but not love, a ticket to anywhere but not to heaven.

Give me a desire to seek the wealth of my heavenly kingdom, for it will never lose value or pass away.

Amen.

Dear heavenly Father, forgive us if our morality is divorced from our piety. Forgive us if we carry around moral vanity.

Show us that successful businesses in the true sense are based on biblical morality.

May we be aware that our morality often shows in the attitude we have toward the people we dislike.

Lord, teach us that what we glory in reveals our morality, and that, though religions and beliefs differ, true morality is everywhere the same.

Show us that our love for you and for others is based on the morality of a true relationship with you through Jesus Christ.

Amen.

MORTALITY

Dear Lord, your Word says that our lives pass like swift ships at sea, like clouds racing across the sky, and like their shadows running over the ground. Your Word says that we are temporary as the grass in the pastures and as brief as flowers that bloom.

Lord, every falling leaf whispers that we are mortal, that our days are fast and few. Even in the hearts of those who love us, where we make the strongest impressions, we must die.

We thank you that the grave is not the end for your children. For, at the sound of the resurrection trumpet we shall rise to a blemishless immortality, freed from every chain of this mortal coil.

There, with you, good-byes will never be said, tears will never fall, hearts never feel pain, and fear be no more.

Amen.

MOTHER

Dear Lord, if we could compress all suns into one candlelight, all oceans into one drop of water, all flowers into one rose, all great literature into one book, all beautiful music into one song, all sunsets into one blaze of glory, all love into a single glance, it would be a true mother's heart.

Amen.

MUSIC

Dear Father, I thank you for music—the magic of sound, the intoxication of the senses, the universal kinship with all mankind, the expression of all the inarticulate nostalgia of the human race.

I thank you for music, expressing every mood of the heart, every yearning of the soul, which in its highest moments becomes an act of communion.

Dear Lord, we hear music in nature—in wind singing through the trees, in the surf rioting on the shore, in thunder beating distant drums, in bird song, and in a thousand other ways.

I thank you for music from the heart and the soul—in the harmonies of a choir, in the singing strings of a violin, in a piano's articulate complexions.

I thank you, most of all, for the music of being in harmony with you—for the vibrations of joy, the grace notes of praise, the soul-warming melodies of redemption through Christ.

Amen.

NAME OF JESUS

Dear Lord, I thank you for the name of Jesus.

It is sweeter than exquisite music and stronger than irresistible power.

It lisps in cradle lullabies and lingers in old memories. It glistens in our tears and rings the bells of our hopes.

His name will never die. It will blaze long after the glitter of glamour tarnishes. It will outlast the pyramids and be unfading long after stars grow cold.

His name will rise in crescendos from every quivering harp and ascend with every jubilant voice till every knee shall bend and every tongue confess that he is Lord, the Mighty God, the Prince of Peace.

Amen.

NATURE

Dear Creator, I thank you for the beauty of nature and the wonder it instills.

I thank you for the way a rose flames on a stem, the way a cloud is afire at sunset, the way a wave curls upon the shore, the way sunrise gilds a mountain peak.

I thank you for the way a redwood towers in cool mists, the way a waterfall trips down a stairway of stone.

I thank you for the way a tern migrates, the way a canary sings, the way wind rustles through trees, the way a river flows to the sea.

I thank you for the mysteries of atoms and stars, of light and sound, and the way rainbows gleam within diamonds.

For all the wonders you have made and for all that thrills my soul, I give you thanks.

Amen.

NEIGHBOR

Father in heaven, my neighbor is more than a mere person living next door. He is a person with dreams, hopes, yearnings, and needs. He is an environment in which I live, a mirror in which I see myself.

May I love my neighbor as myself and be as concerned with his hopes and hurts as much as I am over my own.

Amen.

NEW BIRTH

Dear God of my salvation, through the death of Jesus in my place you have cleansed me from my sins and have given me the gift of a new life in Christ. You have justified me by the declaration of your grace, and I am born again.

I am born to freedom, to joy, to ultimate victory. I am born to a new name, a new family, a new relationship, and a new hope. I am part of the royal family through Christ who loved me and gave his life for me.

I have a new song, a new message, and a new responsibility to represent a new truth to others.

When, at last, shadows creep into this vale of tears, and the sun sinks into the west, this new life by faith shall find fulfillment beyond the highest aspirations of my soul in that wonderful world to come.

Amen.

Father in heaven, as this new day dawns, and shadows of night slink away, and the sun gilds the distant hills, we ask that you be with us.

This day is filled with the unknown. Hopes may be dashed, suffering may meet us, disappointment may dampen the spirit. It may be filled with pleasantness, with victory, with new friendships, with opportunity to help someone in need.

Whatever this day holds for us, we commit it to you an hour at a time to be and to do our best.

When its hours are finished, the sun sinks in the west, and night's shadows steal in, may our conscience be guileless, our regrets nonexistent, and our sleep without a care.

Amen.

NEW YEAR

Dear Lord, like trails in unfamiliar territory, new tomorrows stretch before us. Lest, in the thorny underbrush we lose our way, be our Guide.

When we grope through the gloom of failure, support us. When we stand on the peak of acclaim, humble us lest we become inflated beyond what we are.

When we stumble into tangled swamps of powerful temptations, rescue us.

Lead us into lush vales of nourishment and along sunlit streams of contentment lest we become dispirited and bitter.

When our hearts ache for love, make us lavish in giving it away, and it will return to knock at our doors a hundredfold.

In our search for peace, show us that, when pearled with tears, our search is the most elegant.

Teach us the beauty of simplicity and that all great things are built on this foundation.

May we cherish each passing hour and weigh it as if it were our last.

When we come to the end of the trail and look back, may we see we never walked alone.

Amen.

OBEDIENCE

Dear great Lawgiver, may we obey you out of love, not out of coercion.

All your commands are reflections of your divine nature. They are holy, wise, and for your glory and for our good.

May our obedience never be a slavish subservience to a tyrant, but an eager willingness to serve in response to your love expressed through Jesus Christ.

Lord, only in obedience to your commands can we find peace of heart and happiness of life.

Amen.

OLD AGE

Dear Lord, when I grow old, wrinkled, and gray . . . and my eyes dim, my hearing fails, and my memory cannot recall clearly, be with me.

Should I be embarrassed about my appearance, may I remember that I can be lovely inside and that is what I really am.

If I should become invisible to the younger generation and mope in my loneliness, be my comfort.

Give me enough grace for each day, and enough strength to do my little tasks.

Grant me patience when the hours are long, and may I not be bitter with those whose lot in life has been blessed.

Give me a bright hope for each day I linger here—a hope that does not dim though all earthly lights seem far away.

When I lie down to my last sleep, carry me away to heaven where I shall be restored to the fullest sense of eternal youth.

Amen.

OMNIPOTENCE

Dear God of all power, you are all-powerful!

You created a hundred billion galaxies out of nothing.

You created the atom and its wondrous ways.

You made the world of nature with all its life.

You made us in your image, destined for high things.

In our day-to-day living, may we feel a touch of your power to help us overcome temptation, mediocrity, selfishness, and lack of love.

Fill us with your might that we may be all that we have the capacity to become. In Jesus' name.

Amen.

OMNIPRESENCE

Dear God, you are present everywhere. There is no place where you are not. In the atom's heart, with the farthest star—you are there.

You are within us—the inner world where we sing, where we weep, where we hope and despair, where we dream, and where we are disappointed.

You are with us in the humiliating world of rejection, the world of the invasion of disease and of the gray shadow of loneliness.

You are with us when we are happy and when we love . . . when we sing and laugh, and when we have good health.

We are never alone, O God. We cannot escape you.

May we feel and sense your presence all the days of our lives till we see you face-to-face.

Amen.

OMNISCIENCE

Dear God of all knowledge, you know all things!

All thoughts, all circumstances, all events, all words—you have known them from eternity past.

You knew all about each one of us before we were born. Before you, we are transparent. Nothing is hid from you.

You know our strengths and weaknesses. You know our hopes and despairs. You know our dreams and their shattering. You know our caring and our selfishness.

May a sense of your "all-knowingness" change the way we feel, think, and act.

Amen.

Dear heavenly Father, I come to this pew in search of peace to quiet the discord of my daily life. I come to worship your person, to obtain your grace, and your salvation. I come to find relief for the agony in my heart and to find comfort for my sorrow. I come because I am fearful about life, about those close to me, about dying.

Create in me a hunger for the Word of life so my soul can be nourished. Light again the lamp of my hope; shore up my trust in your promises.

In this pew, may I feel the thrill of worship. Fill my heart with gratitude, and may I leave this place renewed in spirit.

Amen.

Dear Father, I know that no one can unwind the clock to bring back the past, or resurrect days that are buried in yesteryear.

Each day I live, I add to the past and subtract from the future.

In my reservoir of memory are stored my days: days of youthful adventure and aspirations; days of middle-age concerns; days of the brittle uncertainties of old age.

The wild oats of disobedience I have sown, the blooming flowers of life I have planted, and the good and evil, the hates and harmonies—all are woven into the lives of others.

Forgive me the sins of my past years when I was far less than I could be.

Lord, help me to learn from my past instead of having it consume me. May I remember from your Word that through the cross of Christ you have buried my sins in the depths of the sea.

Amen.

PATIENCE

Dear Father, in our hurried and harried lives in this day of instant gratification, give us patience to work for the finer ideals of mind and soul that do not become obsolete.

May we be careful to note that a lack of energy is often mistaken for patience and that it can be a minor form of despair disguised as virtue.

Your Word says that you are long-suffering with us. May we also be long-suffering with ourselves and with others.

Amen.

PATRIOTISM

Father of freedom, we thank you for our country and for our freedoms symbolized by our flag.

Dear Lord, prevent a nationalistic egotism from invading our true patriotism, for people everywhere have a natural right to love their country.

Forgive us if we ever feel superior to those in other lands, where the culture and language may differ; for people are the same everywhere. Father, you loved all people everywhere and sent your Son to die for all.

Remind us that we, as your children, are citizens of heaven, our true homeland. May our Christian patriotism never waver or wane for our high calling and for our home above.

Amen.

PEACE OF MIND

Dear Lord of peace, give us peace of mind as well as the mind of peace.

Teach us the importance of life's central things, and to change what we can and accept the rest.

Help us not to get too upset over mysteries that have no earthly answers.

May we look over the high walls of cultural prejudices and see another's point of view.

Lord, make our love unconditional to all, and help us know that slights and insults that come our way are not as significant as our reaction to them.

Today, may we understand that we are all traveling together in space on a dot called earth, and we only have a moment with our companions.

God of peace, today, give us that peace that passes all understanding through Jesus Christ, our Savior.

Amen.

PERFECTIONIST

Dear Lord, forgive me for being so hard on myself and on others because I expect perfection in everybody and in everything.

Help me relax more. Relieve me from the daily stress and accompanying guilt that I live with every day.

Help me laugh at insignificant things and events that are minor in nature.

Show me that no one is perfect and everything on earth is flawed.

May I do my best at whatever I do but not ruin my health, peace of mind, or relationships with others because I demand so much.

As I walk in an imperfect world, may I look up to the only one who is perfect, who alone can give rest of soul.

Amen.

Father, give us clear heads and common sense as we grope through the maze of troubling questions.

Lord, as long as we are on earth, we will be plagued by questions that have no answers.

What we cannot understand may we commit to you, for within your eternal being lie the answers to all things.

Guide us day by day with the light of your Holy Spirit. Help us to live a day at a time in complete trust in your providence.

Amen.

PERSEVERANCE

Dear Lord, so often the road is long and uphill, and I get weary. So often opposition faces me at every turn. So often I want to give up on things that I must do, and even on life itself.

Lord Jesus, you persevered on the cross for my sins that you might redeem me.

Help me, like Paul of old, to press toward the goal line for the trophy of my high calling in Christ Jesus.

Give me daily strength to keep on, for tomorrow may bring the answer. Perhaps, around the next bend in the road the goal will be reached.

Help me never to give up doing with is right for myself and for others.

Amen.

PHYSICIAN

Dear Lord, I pray for my doctor. Guide him in his diagnosis, in the surgery room, in his prescription of drugs, for my life is in his hands.

May he see me as a person with fears and many questions. May he enter into my life and feel that my future may be uncertain.

Help me to trust in him to do his best for me, for that itself is healing.

I commit him to you and myself to his hands.

I thank you for the body's gift of healing and also for your divine healing touch.

Amen.

PITY

Lord of all mercy, if our hearts are turned to stone, break them so we can learn the fine art of pity.

If our eyes are used only for our good, relieve our blindness.

Lord, there are millions across the world who are in want of food, who are suffering and in agony, who are passing through sorrow. Help us to have pity for them and extend our hand to help.

Your Word says that you pity those who are your children. May we extend that same pity to those who are not.

Amen.

PLEASURE

Dear Lord, forgive us if we have made pleasure a goal in life rather than a current activity of body, mind, and soul.

Teach us that true pleasure is moral in nature and dies as soon as morality departs.

Lord, we know it is true that all pleasure comes at the price of some pain.

Lord, when life has ended for us, we will reflect that our purest pleasures were in serving you and in helping others.

Help us see that our truest pleasure has as its source our relationship with Christ and that time will not age it, rust corrode it, or fashion change it.

Amen.

POETRY

Dear God of rhyme and rhythm, we thank you for poetry, the passionate love of language, forged slowly, link by link with tears, blood, and sweat; a noble thought seasoned a long time in the garrets of the mind, then brought down, and slowly carved into words, formed with emotion, and polished with affection.

We thank you for the poetry of the Bible, the fragrance of exalted thoughts captured in imagery that lifts the soul into high realms.

Amen.

POVERTY

Dear Father, we pray for those who live on the poverty level through no fault of their own.

Lord, poverty can come from idleness, extravagance, and intemperance. Forgive us if we are guilty of these.

We are aware that poverty often causes virtue to stumble and fall, that it stifles talent and ability, that it often traps the elderly in hunger, neglect, and privation.

Lord, we know that the poor will always be with us. We pray for them. Fulfill their needs. Restore their self-respect. Help them in Jesus' name.

Amen.

PRAYER

Dear Lord, I thank you that through the wonder of prayer I can be in personal communication with the God of the universe.

I do not always need to pray audibly. Prayer to you can take many forms. It can be a meditation, a sense of awe, of worship. It can be confession, praise, or thanksgiving. It is simply the communion of the heart with its God.

Teach me that it is better to have a right heart without words than mere words without a heart.

Help me to realize that thoughts alone can be a prayer when the soul is on its knees.

Help my prayers to be the keys of the morning and the locks of the night.

Lord, show me that true prayer is based on love and exists in every beautiful and noble emotion that lifts our souls heavenward.

In the name of Jesus, our Advocate, we pray.
Amen.

PREJUDICE

Dear Father in heaven, forgive us for being ignorant and for peddling, without good reason, our prejudices. Forgive us for our jaundiced eye without sufficient warrant and for believing so firmly that about which we know the least.

Forgive us for thinking that we think when we are only realigning our biases.

Help us to get rid of prejudice by understanding and becoming empathetic.

May we break out of the walls of our own experiences and enter those of others.

May we love without preference as you loved us.

May we demolish our fortifications of prejudice and build bridges across the rivers that separate us.

Amen.

PRESIDENT

Dear Father, we pray for our president. It is often lonely at the top. The great responsibility of leading our nation rests heavily upon his shoulders.

Give him wisdom and diplomacy in the great pressures of international relations. Give him courage to face down fearful forces of tyranny and enslavement.

May he possess in every consideration and decision unblemished integrity.

Grant him clarity of mind to sift through thorny issues and courage to stand for what is right.

In times of war or peace, of recession or prosperity, of unity or anarchy, give him personal strength, the support of his cabinet and congress.

Most of all, may he seek your wisdom and the affirming sense of your presence in all that he does.

Amen.

PRIDE

Dear Lord of humility, forgive us for those times when we have overestimated ourselves because of self-centeredness.

Forgive us for hiding behind a mask called "pride," for it only covers our faults.

Teach us that there is only a step between a proud person's glory and disgrace.

Lord, show us true humility of heart, and not the merely external show of it. Help us to see the correct estimation of ourselves.

From your Word, may we learn that we can have a true pride in country, in achievements, in families, but that the greatest pride is found in relationship with you.

Amen.

PRIORITIES

Dear Lord, there are a thousand things and obligations
that call for first place in our daily living.

Give us the wisdom to separate the important from
the unimportant. Help us set aside all that caters to
selfish interest.

Help us to set in first place those things that will
outlast us as a legacy to those who follow.

May we always set you as first priority. Then, in the
end, all else will seem secondary.

Amen.

PRISONERS

Dear Lord of compassion, there are thousands imprisoned for all kinds of reasons. We do not understand all the circumstances that led to their crimes. There are, no doubt, those who are innocent.

Many are experiencing great frustration of mind and spirit. Most do not know your forgiveness and a peace of heart.

As they serve their sentences, may they find life in Christ and the strength to live each day until release.

Make us realize that the greatest prisons are the bars of fear, guilt, anger, and hate.

Be with the families of those imprisoned. Give them courage to go on. Spare them from excessive hardship. May they feel your love.

Amen.

PROSPERITY

Our heavenly Father, forgive us if we have made prosperity the only aim in life.

If we have prosperity, may it become a servant to be used for the good and not a tyrant to make us slaves.

Lord, we may learn many things from prosperity, but we learn more through adversity.

May we remember that prosperity may make many friends, but adversity tries them.

Teach us the warning that a prosperous person is never sure if he is loved for himself or not.

Make our souls prosperous. Give us inner wealth, for it is immune to changing values. Save us from selfishness, pride, and arrogance. Help us remember those who have nothing.

Lord Jesus, you were poor in material things, yet you came to make us immensely rich through your salvation, for which we give you thanks.

Amen.

PROTECTION

Father, danger lies in ambush down every road and street. Disease lurks within our bodies and wrong intents within our hearts. We are surrounded by physical and spiritual dangers.

As we go about our daily tasks, protect us from danger wherever it may be.

Protect us from the wiles of the evil one, and from our own vices and weaknesses.

Be our Good Shepherd along the trails of life where dangers hide. Calm our fears, for we are your children, and you walk with us each day.

Amen.

PROVIDENCE

Dear Father, your ways and thoughts are as far above ours as the heavens are above the earth. In your deep and eternal wisdom lie answers to life's questions.

Yet, so many of life's great troubles are due to the willful sins of the human race.

Grant us faith in your providence that what you allow to happen is often for our good. May we not get unduly involved in the interpretation of your providence.

You care for the sparrow and the lily from season to season. Your Word says that we are worth more to you than many sparrows. You will care for us.

For every trial, give grace to help us bear it. Though we do not understand why so many things happen, your eternal purposes work through all creation for your glory and, in the end, for our good.

Amen.

Dear Lord, I am nervous before this speech. I've tried to be well prepared and organized. I want to be careful in my expression of language so that I may be clear to all present.

Above all, may I have researched well and be truthful in all I say.

May the subject that I have chosen be helpful to my listeners, and may their lives be better for listening.

I surrender myself to you. Speak through me, for only then can I be truly effective.

Amen.

QUARRELS

Father of peace, help us see that no one is immune from a quarrel. It only takes one person to start, but it would not last long if only one was at fault. Usually weakness and fault are on both sides of a quarrel.

Father, we know it is important to be strong if important truth is at stake. May our words and feelings never be stronger than they need to be.

Grant us a willingness to understand the other person's point of view, for it may contain much truth.

May our point of view be accurate, may our attitude be considerate, and may our heart be loving. Lord, if we must be different, may we not be difficult.

Amen.

QUITTING

Dear Lord of strength, at times, it is so easy to quit because I am tired or discouraged, because I face opposition, or I have a change in thinking and feeling.

May I always keep what I have promised if it is at all possible. May I make a practice of integrity before you, to myself, and to others.

The world would have been so much poorer if Rembrandt, Handel, Beethoven, Milton, Shakespeare, and Lincoln would have quit midway.

The world would have never known your grace if Jesus had quit.

Give me persistence to reach worthwhile goals, but the wisdom to stop if I am on the wrong track.

Amen.

RECONCILIATION

Dear Lord of peace and reconciliation, sometimes in life, we are estranged from others. Tempers flare, hot words flame, insults are traded, and the rupture may last for years.

May we be the first to attempt a reconciliation, for we may have been unkind, uncompassionate, selfish, stubborn, and unchristian.

May we not be afraid to apologize, to ask forgiveness, and to come to an understanding, even if we may be in the right.

There is nothing more discordant in life than deliberate distance, and nothing more beautiful than living in harmonious nearness.

Your Word says that we are reconciled to you through the death of Jesus Christ. Help us to be reconciled to others through the example of Christ.

Amen.

REJECTION

Lord of compassion, sometimes we are wounded lifelong through rejection. It often cuts to the bone and leaves scar tissue through the years.

Help us understand that often the one who rejects us is troubled, wounded, abused, and the rejection is not due to us.

Show us that our value is not measured by the estimate of others, but by the infinite love of Calvary.

Should we be rejected for Christ's sake, help us rejoice, for our reward will await us in heaven.

May we accept others as they are and love them into your kingdom.

Amen.

RENEWAL

Dear Lord of renewal, may the sun and rain of the Holy Spirit change the decay of autumn and cold of winter into a resurrection of new and abundant life.

Our minds have often focused on all that is temporary and have forgotten those values that outlast time.

Our hearts have been chilled with the coldness of indifference, and we have turned inward into self-centeredness.

Renew us like showers of spring across the deserts of our neglect.

Ignite our minds with new ideals, inflame our hearts with new hope, set our feet on highways of new purpose.

We pray in the name of Jesus.

Amen.

REPENTANCE

Dear Father of forgiveness, like prodigals we roamed far countries of fanciful illusions in search of meaning and hope and discovered that when we returned home to you, we found them.

Like a pious Pharisee, we paraded our fake superiority over those of lesser station and found that we masked our own sinfulness.

Like a doubting Thomas, we fail to take you at your word and demand sensory proof.

Forgive us our sins. Cleanse us from all wrongs we have committed. Make us pure, clean, and fresh in your sight.

Amen.

RESENTMENT

Dear heavenly Father, forgive us for locking rusted resentments in safe-deposit boxes of memory as if they were bars of gold.

Forgive us for turning a cold shoulder when we should have extended a warm greeting.

Forgive us for losing our temper instead of preserving our temperance.

Forgive us for being suspicious without reason and judging others in the dim light of our imperfect selves.

Help us see life through another's eyes if at all possible. May we learn to love each other without attaching conditions, for life is short and we only at best have a moment with friends and families.

Amen.

RESPONSIBILITY

Dear Lord, pull up the poisonous weeds of irresponsibility, selfishness, disloyalty from the garden of my life so that I may not be sapped from becoming what I must be.

May my word be my bond, my promise my undeviating intention, and my dependability the constant practice of my life.

Help me through the power of the Holy Spirit.
Amen.

RESTLESSNESS

Dear Lord, often a vague, indefinite something gnaws at the edges of my serenity, and I feel frazzled and threadbare in spirit.

Sometimes I feel like a lost ship at sea, tossing on waves of doubt.

Lord, your Word says that you will keep me in perfect peace if my mind is fixed on you.

Lord, be my polestar on the turbulent waters of my earthly voyage.

Give me that unperturbable serenity that comes from absolute faith in your promise to me.

Exchange my restlessness for the rest of forgiven sins and a firm hope for all the future.

Amen.

RESTORATION

Dear Good Shepherd, restore the malnourishment in my soul with the energy of the Bread of Life.

Quench my thirsty yearnings for deeper and purer springs with the Water of Life.

Rescue me from the tangled brush of hopeless swamps and point my feet toward paths of righteousness.

When I feel downtrodden and depressed, fill my cup to the brim with joy.

When I near the end of my journey on earth, alleviate my uncertainties with a sense of your presence.

Restore me with your goodness and mercy, and in that city of light, let me reside forever.

Amen.

REVENGE

Dear Father, your Word says that revenge belongs to you and that some day you will repay.

Spare us the temptation of always trying to get even, for when we do, we always lower ourselves beneath those who wronged us.

Show us that the best way to avenge ourselves is not to resemble those who hurt us.

Instead, give us the grace to turn the other cheek, to walk the second mile, and to return kindness for insult and injury, and, in so doing, possibly turn our enemies into friends.

Amen.

REWARD

Father, if we do a good work and do not receive a reward or recognition, may we not be bitter or feel ignored, for you will reward us in the end.

Lord, remind us of how often the greatest reward is to do things secretly and be found out by accident.

Teach us that love has the greatest reward if we give it away. It will return with its hands full of dividends.

Lord, your Word says that we will be rewarded according to our deeds when we get to heaven. May we remember that all trophies on earth lose their luster, but what you give us will keep its shine forever.

Amen.

RICHES

Father of true wealth, forgive us if we have made riches an end in life rather than an instrument to be used.

Show us that riches without your love are only temporary expediencies and that their real worth is when they become blessings to others.

Teach us that health, freedom, and self-esteem are riches, but that love is the richest gift of all.

Lord, contentment lies not in money but in the heart, for anyone can be content with little, and none has contentment when the search for it is only in wealth.

Lord, oftentimes, riches have wings, and there is a burden getting them, fear in keeping them, guilt in abusing them, and sorrow in losing them.

Show us from your Word that true wealth is in Christ Jesus and that it is without parallel. It is safe from robbers, not subject to loss or devaluation, and never probated.

Amen.

RUNAWAY CHILD

Dear Lord, watch over a child who has run away from home. Perhaps the home was too abusive. Perhaps the glitter of the world was too tempting.

We know the great anxiety of many parents whose children have run away. Help them, we pray.

Protect these children who leave home to find peace and happiness elsewhere. May they be reunited to their families in a wonderful reconciliation. In Jesus' name.

Amen.

SACRIFICE

Dear Father, teach us by your Spirit that we can truly sacrifice no more than we love, and that we love no more than we are willing to sacrifice.

Amen.

SADNESS

Dear Lord, I am feeling sad, and I don't know why.

Under this dark cloud I have looked for a rim of gold, but there is none.

A deep emptiness is within me, a lonely ache I cannot explain.

I pray that you will reveal yourself to me. May I experience the warmth of your comforting presence. Fold me in your arms, and may I hear the beat of your heart for me.

Like Paul, help me to sing, if possible, in this prison of my sadness. In this unwanted gloom, help me to trust your irrevocable promise that you will never leave me nor forsake me.

Amen.

SAFETY

Dear Great Protector, in danger on the trailway, the roadway, the freeway, and the airway — protect us.

From danger seen and unseen, foreknown and unforeknown, latent or obvious — protect us.

In carefulness or carelessness, war or peace, living or dying — protect us.

In work or leisure, at home or travel, sickness or health — protect us.

You are our Shepherd; we, your sheep. You are strong; we are defenseless. You see the future; we, only the present. Watch over us, because we are your children.

Amen.

Dear Creator, we thank you for the birth of spring,
dressed in robes of freshness and beauty.

We thank you for summer, for ripening fruit, for
golden harvests, for cattle browsing in green meadows,
for fledging birds trying new wings.

We thank you for autumn, for turning of leaves, for
migrating birds, for a chill wind rustling through brown
cornfields.

We thank you for winter when nature lies hushed and
asleep under blankets of white.

Lord, in the seasons of our lives—in the spring of
youth, in the summer of middle age, in the autumn of
declining years, in the winter of laying aside our tools
and falling asleep in your arms—be with us.

Amen.

SELF-CENTEREDNESS

Dear Lord, forgive us for being occupied with either our self-pride or self-contempt.

Become the center of our being so that from this fountain of compassion streams of living water will flow across the dry sands of others' lives.

May we be Christ-centered. We are but tools in his hands. The dream and design, the power and giftedness are not in the tool, but in the heart of the great Designer.

Stop us from bowing down to this unworthy idol of self. May we commit ourselves into your hands, for we are of little value apart from your presence and power.

Amen.

SELF-ESTEEM

Dear heavenly Father, help us to base our self-esteem on what we are through Christ.

May we work out this exalted position in our lives:

That when we are self-centered, we cannot be others-centered.

That when we are selfish, we cannot be altruistic.

That if we disrespect and undervalue ourselves, so will others.

That if we do not love ourselves as we are, we cannot expect others to do the same.

We pray that we may ever remember that we have a royal position in Christ, and that in him we are complete and have inestimable value.

Grant us the grace to work this out in our lives.

Amen.

SENSES

Dear Lord, we thank you for vivid impressions garnered through our sensory organs:

The scent of a rose, the aroma of a clover field in bloom, a favorite perfume, the musk of the sea, and a hundred odors that bring back special memories of long-gone days.

We thank you for sight, the face of a mother, a mountain scarfed in clouds, a bee in the sun, a rainbow against a storm cloud, a sun sinking beyond western hills.

We thank you for the gift of hearing, the sweet voice of music, the lilting laughter of children, the rustle of wind through leaves, the deep bass of thunder, the words of love.

We thank you for the gift of touch, for shapes and textures, hot and cold, smooth and rough.

We thank you for taste, for all the savory delicacies that tempt our tongues.

We thank you in Jesus' name.

Amen.

SERVICE

Dear Lord of the harvest, the fields are golden, the winter is coming, our sickles need sharpening.

Dear Lord, the world is waiting for the message of life as found in the sacred Scriptures.

Bodies are broken and famished, spirits are defeated, hearts are hungry for caring and love.

Lord, the highest calling in the world is to serve the needs of others.

As Jesus washed the disciples' feet, may we symbolically wash one another's.

We thank you, our Lord, for becoming a servant that we might become members of the royal family.

Amen.

SERVICE CLUB

Father in heaven, we ask that your presence be with this
service club today.

Guide our discussion and decision making, stimulate
our conversation, and may we grow closer to one
another.

May we be effective in our outreach to the
community and an example for morality in all our
transactions.

We ask in your name.

Amen.

SIMPLICITY

Father, help us sort out all trivia that steals precious time, that numbs our senses, that cripples us from climbing mountains of greater values.

Show us the joy of solitude, the music of silence, the healing of the quiet.

Lord, in this complex age of countless commercials, of flaunted vice, of a thousand things that compete for our attention, help us to be still and search for the serenity of simplicity.

Help us remember that the greatest beauty in the world is simple.

We thank you for the simple message of salvation by faith.

May the magic of simplicity touch our lives, for it is the surest way to peace and happiness.

Amen.

SIN

Dear Great Forgiver, no sin is small, for it is against a holy and infinite God, and it has great consequences.

Often, Lord, we are punished by our sins in body, mind, and spirit.

May we remember that God forgives our sins, but many times our nervous system won't.

We thank you that Jesus Christ took upon himself our sins on the cross and bore the punishment for them.

Lord, we confess our sins, knowing that you will forgive them through Christ, by faith, and that we will be cleansed.

Amen.

SLANDER

Dear Lord, no one is safe from the sinister tongue of slander, and often the worthiest are the most injured by it.

Lord, the swift feet of slander cannot be outrun. People want to believe the worst about others.

Give us the strength to be silent, for to reply fuels the fire.

Grant us the courage to do what is right and to find security and contentment within our own being.

Give us also the courage to speak up when it is proper lest silence be the accusation of guilt.

Help us to live the humble, dedicated Christian life, and in the end you will judge every person according to the deeds performed.

Amen.

SORROW

Dear God of comfort, comfort me in these memories that mist my eye, in this dull ache that gnaws my heart, in the silent sobbing of my grief.

Lord, I grope for words to express what I feel, but there are no words.

Through my long days and sleepless nights may I sense the reality of your presence.

For the many questions that defy answers, be my strength.

Your Word states that Jesus was acquainted with grief, for he was called the Man of Sorrows.

Be my comfort in this very personal loss.

Amen.

Dear Lord, in the stadium of the Christian life, may we put on the protective gear of your Word lest we be disabled by the crippling jolts of our daily contacts.

Develop our moral and spiritual muscles with the gymnastics of study and prayer so we can successfully compete against spiritual forces that are against us.

Be our coach. Whip us into enthusiasm to win at all costs because we are representing the team of the Christian life.

May we not have our eyes on the trophies of time, but look toward the "well done" when we walk through the gates of pearl.

Amen.

STEALING

Father, forgive us for stealing our own or another's time.

Forgive us for stealing another's reputation by a bit of slander or lying.

Forgive us for stealing an employer's money by not doing our job the way we ought.

Forgive us for taking advantage of another's weakness by pressing a bargain too far.

Forgive us for neglecting your Word, for not praying for one another, for not loving, for not helping someone carrying a heavy load, for that is also stealing.

Lord, there are a thousand seemingly innocent ways of stealing. May we be givers instead of takers.

Amen.

STRESS

Dear Lord of peace, we are bombarded from every corner by stress in our modern life. Life is so complex at times that we are bowed by the burden of it.

Bring a center of calm in the vortex of pressure. Help us to ignore what is unimportant and not to be carried away by the insignificant.

Help us to simplify our lives, for all things beautiful are simple.

Give us a sense of control, of peace, of inner rest lest we pay in health and shorter lives. Help us through Jesus Christ.

Amen.

STUBBORNNESS

Father in heaven, often, we know that our stubbornness is based on ignorance of the facts.

Lord, each of us is entitled to a viewpoint. Help us to be open-minded, to search out all the facts before we draw conclusions.

Teach us that it is a virtue to admit we are wrong and a vice to stubbornly defend what we know is not true.

As your children, may we be compassionate in heart, for that is the spirit of Christ.

Amen.

STUDENT

Dear Great Teacher, my lessons are difficult, my teachers demanding, and I am stressed with some of my peers and with my parents.

Give me the will and the strength to plod ahead a day at a time till I make graduation, for there is no glory in ignorance.

Increase my mental appetite. May I never fail to see an aura of wonder in everything on earth.

In studies that I am not adept at, give me patience and persistence. May I never shrink from that which is difficult, for life is full of difficulties.

May I do my best, even if I do not make the grade, for failing is not necessarily wrong, but failing to try is.

When I graduate, above the ceremonies within the school, may I wear the cap and gown of your honor and receive the diploma of your "well done!"

Amen.

SUCCESS

Dear Lord of true success, teach us that we win by
losing; we live by dying; we move forward on our
knees; we win by giving up; we are masters by serving;
we are freed by being bound; we receive by giving; we
become strong in weakness; we discover resurrection in
dying; we find our lightest load in carrying the cross; we
find happiness by giving it away; we belong to royalty
by being servants.
Amen.

SUFFERING

Dear God, when pain racks our bodies, when tears scald our cheeks, when our minds grope for answers, when our hearts lose all hope, be with us.

Show us that the blackest night flashes the brightest stars, and the loveliest rainbow is pinned against the darkest storm cloud.

Lord, sometimes you allow the fires of pain and suffering to burn the dross and to imprint the design of the Great Designer on the pottery of our lives.

Lord, we know that suffering reveals our inner strengths and weaknesses. It is a mirror that reflects our characters.

If we suffer for your sake, let us be glad, for great is our reward in heaven.

When the dark night is the longest, pain the most severe, the outcome the most hopeless, may our faith never fail because it is anchored to the Rock of Ages.

Show us that when our shadows are the darkest, your light is the brightest.

Amen.

SUICIDE

Father of life, few of us know about the black despair within the heart of the one who contemplates suicide.

May we not be judgmental of the person who seeks a way out of life because there is fear of living it. There are so many contributing causes that we do not understand.

Somehow, may such a person find through your power an answer to life.

Undergird him with your consoling presence. Take away the hopelessness and the fear. Give peace of mind and heart through Jesus Christ.

Amen.

SUNDAY SCHOOL CLASS

Dear Lord of all learning, the members of this class are before me. Help me to sense their personal needs. May I be sensitive to their deepest feelings.

If there is doubt, may I illustrate faith; if there is fear, may I show the way to peace; if there is a desire to learn, may I impart knowledge; if there is need for repentance, may I point to the way to the cross.

Think through my mind. Speak through my tongue vividly and clearly so that all of us together will experience a spiritual metamorphosis through the Holy Spirit.

Amen.

SUPERIORITY

Dear Lord, if we are tempted to parade any sense of superiority over others, remind us that we are all made of the same common clay.

Yet, in your sight, we are of equal worth for our value is measured by the blood of the cross.

Lord, some are superior by way of giftedness or ability, but we are all created in your image.

Forgive us for wearing false pride as if it were designer clothes.

May we always keep our chin up but our nose at a reasonable level.

Amen.

SURRENDER

Dear Lord, teach me the paradox of winning by surrendering.

We know we are bound to defeat if we fight with our own inadequate human resources.

We surrender to your power, to your love, to your plan for our lives. Only then are we sure of winning.

May we discover that if we surrender our weakness, we are made strong. If we surrender our resentment, we are able to love. If we surrender our doubts, we have faith. If we surrender our fears, we have serenity.

Lord, we surrender all that we are and all that we have to you. Conquer us and subdue us till we have total victory through Christ our Lord.

Amen.

TACT

Dear Father, so often I blurt out things I deeply feel without thought for others' feelings.

Help me remember to weigh my words as carefully as a jeweler weighs diamonds.

Father, may I not mistake cowardice or weakness for tact. May I neither be silent when I ought to speak.

May the Holy Spirit guide my sensitivity for others as well as my honesty toward myself.

Amen.

TALENT

Great Giver of Gifts, you have gifted us each with a latent talent at birth. It is our responsibility to discover and develop it.

Dear Lord, a talent is to be used to glorify you, to minister to others, and it is attached a great responsibility.

We dedicate this talent to you to enrich, help, and bless the lives of others.

Amen.

TEACHER

Dear Great Teacher, as I stand before my class, may I realize my great responsibility.

May I be well prepared. May I realize that teaching without inspiring the pupil may be a waste of time.

May I awaken the natural curiosity of the mind to learn more of the subject.

May I awaken the heart to feel strongly about important knowledge.

Lord, this moment, before my class, help me see that I teach more by what I am than by what I will say.

Amen.

TEMPER

Dear Father in heaven, I understand that an acid temper
seldom mellows with age, and that a sharp tongue grows
keener with use.

Lord, I know that a temper is temperament out of
control, and that I lose my temper when I run out of
argument.

May I hold my tongue and say nothing before I say
too much.

Teach me that loss of temper never makes up for the
power of words in their right order.

May the Holy Spirit control my life so that my words
are calm, but firm, truthful, yet loving, uncompromising,
yet understanding.

Amen.

TEMPERANCE

Dear Lord, keep me from anything that injures my body as your temple, my mind as your vehicle to think, my tongue as your organ to speak, my heart as your residence to live in.

Amen.

TEMPTATION

Dear Lord of guidance, temptation comes to everyone in some form or other, and there is no one who cannot be broken down with the right temptation.

Help us to understand others' weaknesses, for if we were subject to the same influences, we also would fall.

Lord, so often the bait is alluring, but the trap is fatal.

Show us from your Word that Christ himself was tempted in all ways that we are, yet he never sinned.

Show us also that if we walk in your light, you will provide a way of escape.

We pray in the power of your Holy Spirit.

Amen.

TESTINGS

Dear Lord, it is hard to endure testing—like gold in the fire, metal on the anvil. Its tensions, stresses, and strains almost break us.

Yet, like Job of old, we may come out of it purified, strengthened, with understanding and empathy.

Your Word states that you will not allow circumstances to destroy us or give that which is above our ability to bear.

Though we may be tried as by fire, may we be as pure gold in your sight.

Amen.

THANKFULNESS

Dear Father, we give you thanks for the wonders of your universe—for the twinkle of a far star, for a waterfall dancing down stairways of stone, for a wave churning through rocks, for mountains heaving massive shoulders against the blue, for sunsets painting Rembrandts with brushes of sunbeams and pigments of vapor.

We give you thanks for Jesus. No one in all history compares with him. He is the Good Shepherd for our straying. He is the Rock of Ages for the quicksand of our doubts. He is the Bread of Life for our soul's hunger. He is the light for our sunless discouragements. He is the peace for our worries. He is the resurrection for our life to come.

When, at last, evening comes, and dark mists roll in, and we, like weary children fall asleep, lift us and carry us up stairways of light to awaken in that golden dawn of eternal life. Lord, in that paradise to come, there will be peace without violence, love without bitterness, joy without melancholy, reunion without parting, and life without dying.

For this we give you thanks.
Amen.

THANKSGIVING PRAYER

Father, for creation, whether a stone or a star, a molecule or a Milky Way, an embryo or an elephant, a rhododendron or a redwood—we give you thanks.

For a sunset flaming, a waterfall tumbling, a mountain heaving massive shoulders against the sky—we give you thanks.

For the way of a bird on the wing, the way of a horse on the run, the way of a fish in the sea—we give you thanks.

For country byways, for cattle on a thousand hills, and homesteads in a thousand valleys—we give you thanks.

For the magic of music, the beauty of brush and pigment, the quintessence of great literature—we give you thanks.

For kind words cheering, for strong arms lifting, for unconditional love accepting—we give you thanks.

For homes, health, and happiness, for the flag rippling in free winds, for a million church steeples pointing to the stars—we give you thanks.

For your promises that know no breaking, your forgiveness that knows no returning, your love that knows no diminishing—we give you thanks. For your comfort under dark skies of loss, for your light in shadowed valleys of fear, for your guidance in wild wildernesses of confusion—we give you thanks.

For bright moments and dim memories, for hearty laughter and welling tears, for all that time and distance cannot erase—we give you thanks.

For Thanksgiving Day, for renewing of family ties (old, new, near, or far), for roast turkey and pumpkin pie—we give you thanks.

For all of life and that of the world to come—we give you thanks.

Amen.

TIME

Father of eternity, you have given to us the gift of time and clocks with which to measure it.

Often, we seek to kill time, but time kills us in the end. We cannot kill time without affecting eternity.

We confess to squandering time, for it never returns.

May we invest our best into each flying minute through your power.

Lord, how mysterious time is! How short! How wonderful!

O God of timelessness, we thank you for life itself, for the privilege of hearing your gospel and for the hope of sharing eternity with you.

Amen.

TONGUE

Dear Lord, forgive us, for sometimes our tongues run away with our brains and get us into all kinds of trouble.

Lord, we write our autobiographies with our tongues, and many times it makes bad reading.

Help us see that our words are symbols of character and are open books that everyone can read.

Because we are your children, may our words be loving, bathed in tenderness, yet firm when necessary, never compromising, and always truthful.

Lord, countless numbers of people are deeply hurt, maimed, and many have died premature deaths because of slander and razor-sharp edges of evil tongues.

May our words and meditations always be acceptable in your sight, for you are our Lord and our Redeemer.

Amen.

TRUTH

Dear God of truth, forgive us for being tempted to
discover that it is easier to change the truth than
ourselves.

Show us that a partial truth when we should tell all is
as bad as falsehood.

Help us always remember that a truth that dis-
courages us is of far greater value than the best of lies.

Jesus said that he is the truth and that if we follow
him, truth would make us free.

May we never hide the truth, for truth, like a lion,
needs no defense.

Amen.

TWILIGHT YEARS

Dear Savior, I am in my twilight years, and I see shades of night stealing over the sky of life.

My work is finished; my life is nearing its close; I await the call to your presence.

May I leave no lingering regrets of the past. May I have set things right with people I have wronged. Forgive me, for I was not always what I could have been. There is no turning back; life is a one-way street.

As I near the end of my journey on earth, fill my heart with great anticipation for that world to come.

May my twilight days turn into the sunrise of eternal dawn where I shall await angel song, the strumming of celestial harps, and the embracing of those I have loved.

Amen.

UNEMPLOYED

Dear Lord, for myself, and for my family, I need adequate and satisfying employment.

My loss of work is affecting my health, my dignity, my self-worth, and my income to care for those I love.

Help me to find that job that will match my talents, my interest, and my financial obligations.

You understand the stresses of hungry mouths, overdue bills, and worry over the future.

I ask in Jesus' name.

Amen.

Dear Lord, so often we languish in defeat. So often we hoist the white flag of surrender.

We have a wonderful message, a great goal, your divine power. I pray that you will help us claim the victory through Christ.

Resurrect us from the decay of our defeatism.

Multiply the loaves and fishes of our inadequacies till we hunger no more. Turn the stale water of our discontent into the new wine of joy.

May the silver streams tumbling from your mountains of mercy wash across the littered flats of our spiritual doldrums.

Help us see Jesus who will give us the victory.

May we see his face—serene as a sunset. May we sense his presence—calming as a lullaby. May we feel his love—tender as a lovely spring day. May we experience his power—strong as the love of a mother.

Amen.

VIRTUE

Dear Father in heaven, we pray that we may personify virtue, for it is its own reward.

May we not give in to our temptations to vice, for it will do us in if it can.

Save us from the misunderstanding that we can become virtuous just because vice tempts us no longer.

Show us that virtue is not merely the absence of vice, but it is much more—it is a positive thing.

May we see that vices hurt us even in our pleasures, but virtues comfort us in our pain.

Deliver us from Satan's temptations, and may virtue be the essence of our lives.

Amen.

WAR

Dear God of peace, spare this land and our lives from the insanity of war.

Spare us from the destruction of cities, the killing of thousands, the maiming of innocent children, the rubble and ruin, and the hopeless misery that follows.

Wherever they are, protect our servicemen and servicewomen in whatever function they perform.

Give us a vision of Jesus, the Prince of Peace, who will give our hearts peace, and then we will have peace on earth.

Amen.

Dear Lord of love, bless this couple as they have been mysteriously united in the bonds of matrimony.

Double their joys and halve their troubles so that both have the strength to handle whatever the future has in store.

Give them health and energy to provide for the necessities of life.

Give them a capacity for tenderness, a strong sense of understanding, and a love that will outlast the tumbled terrain of life.

Give them a willingness to overlook each other's weaknesses and see each other's strengths.

Should children be granted to their lives, may they train them in the fear of God.

In their adversities, may rainbows of hope shine. Within their joys, may love sparkle.

When age settles upon them, and the sunset of life gilds the evening of life with gold, may they still be hand in hand and heart in heart.

Amen.

WILL OF GOD

Dear Lord God, your will is perfect in every way. It proceeds out of your wisdom, holiness, and love.

My will is often self-centered, stubborn, and wrong. My will often chooses what serves my self-interest the best.

Lord, we cannot understand all that happens in history or how you can work your perfect will through it all. Man's will seems to run and to ruin the world, but in eternity we will understand all.

Lord, your will is the way to peace and happiness, to true success, to love, and to service.

This day, work your will into my life that I may be conformed to the image of Christ.

Amen.

WISDOM

Dear Lord, in your Word there is wisdom. If we ask, we will receive from you.

Give us the desire to apply this wisdom to life.

Show us that we need to throw down the iron curtains of fear, prejudice, and ignorance that we have built up.

May we always be generous with truth and love and sparing with condemnation and apathy.

May we not mourn the yesterdays, but give them to your mercy. Give us each new day wrapped in the rose ribbons of the dawn and filled with promise.

Prevent us from squabbling in the empty wilderness of self-centeredness when the land of promise is waiting.

When the last sunset reddens the evening sky, and we hear the call to come home, may we go with great joy.

Amen.

WITNESS

Dear Lord, your Word says that we are walking
witnesses of the gospel of Christ.

We are shining lamps in the night. We are evangels
with a message of life. We are the call of a trumpet in the
battle against sin.

May our hearts be pure, our lives clean. May there be
no uncertainty in our voices.

May our message of life ring true, for we shall be held
accountable as your ambassador in alien fields.

May the Holy Spirit inflame us, your Word instruct
us, your eternal message inspire us, and your
life-changing work give us courage.

We ask in the name of Jesus.

Amen.

WORDS

Dear Lord, long ago King Solomon wrote that a word aptly spoken is like apples of gold in settings of silver.

Teach us the power of a single word. It can lift us to the heights or sink us to the depths. It can free a man or condemn him to death. It can lullaby a baby to sleep or whip a mob to violence.

May we choose our words as we would choose our best friends. May we weigh them as carefully as we would weigh bars of gold.

Lord, our own words will save or condemn us.

We thank you for the revealed Word, for the living Word, and for the true spoken Word.

May we hide your Word in our hearts that we may not sin against you.

Amen.

WORKMANSHIP

Dear Lord, you are the Potter; we are the clay.

Without you, we are formless, useless, and of no value in serving others.

Within our nature, there is much that would mar a lovely vase. We are whirling on the wheel; your hands are shaping us, drawing us up into the lovely shaped object of your plan for us.

Remove from our lives the pebbles, the debris, all that would prevent us from being all that we can be.

In the kiln of test and adversity, burn the dross till we are pure.

Paint upon us the fruits and flowers of the Spirit till we are beautiful.

Use us in your service in whatever way you deem best.

Amen.

WORRY

Dear Lord, we confess to being overly concerned about things over which we have no control.

Lord, we know that worry, doubt, and fear affect our physical, mental, and spiritual health.

Remind us that our body is your temple, and our heart is your residence.

Lord, the greatest star and the smallest hummingbird are under your care. You hold the future and the tomorrows a day at a time.

We give our anxieties to you. Teach us to live one day at a time like the sparrow and the lily.

Amen.

WORSHIP

Dear God of all greatness, we bow before you in
humility and unworthiness.

You are great beyond all comprehension.

You are wise beyond all understanding.

You are eternal beyond all eons of time.

You are holy beyond all known perfection.

You are sovereign beyond all creation.

You alone are worthy of our worship.

Amen.

YESTERDAY

Heavenly Father, yesterday, like all yesterdays, is history and part of memory.

Many yesterdays have passed with regrets, failures, things we should have done differently. We confess them all to you and ask for forgiveness.

Tomorrow is before us, one day at a time. Many tomorrows will be like twisting paths through the brambles. We need your guidance.

Help us bury all the mistakes of our yesterdays and erase them from our memories, for you have forgiven them.

Give us grace to live this day as if it were our last on earth.

Amen.